# The River and the Railroad



WILBUR S. SHEPPERSON SERIES IN NEVADA HISTORY

# The River and

# the Railroad

AN ARCHAEOLOGICAL HISTORY OF RENO

*Mary Ringhoff and*
*Edward J. Stoner*

UNIVERSITY OF NEVADA PRESS | *Reno & Las Vegas*

WILBUR S. SHEPPERSON SERIES
IN NEVADA HISTORY

*Series Editor: Michael Green*

NEVADA HUMANITIES

This publication is made possible in part by a grant from Nevada Humanities, a state program of the National Endowment for the Humanities.

University of Nevada Press, Reno, Nevada 89557 USA

Manufactured in the United States of America
Design by Kathleen Szawiola

*Library of Congress Cataloging-in-Publication Data*
Ringhoff, Mary, 1974-
The river and the railroad : an archaeological history of Reno / Mary Ringhoff and Edward J. Stoner.
p. cm. — (Wilbur S. Shepperson series in Nevada history)
Includes bibliographical references and index.
ISBN 978-0-87417-843-2 (hardcover : alk. paper)
1. Reno (Nev.)—Antiquities. 2. Archaeology and history—Nevada—Reno. 3. Excavations (Archaeology)—Nevada—Reno. 4. Material culture—Nevada—Reno. 5. Reno (Nev.)—Social life and customs. 6. Reno (Nev.)—History.
I. Stoner, Edward J. (Edward Joseph), 1955-
II. Title. III. Title: Archaeological history of Reno.
F849.R4R56 2011
979.3'55—dc22 2010033692

The paper used in this book is a recycled stock made from 30 percent post-consumer waste materials, certified by FSC, and meets the requirements of American National Standard for Information Sciences—Permanence of Paper for Printed Library Materials, ANSI/NISO Z39.48-1992 (R2002). Binding materials were selected for strength and durability.

FIRST PRINTING
20 19 18 17 16 15 14 13 12 11
5 4 3 2 1

# Contents

# Illustrations

FIGURES

MAPS

# Preface

This book is about the sites unearthed during a large-scale archaeological study in downtown Reno. As part of the archaeological research team for the Reno Transportation Rail Access Corridor (ReTRAC) project, we had the opportunity not only to participate in the largest public works endeavor ever undertaken in Reno, but also to explore the evidence of thousands of years of human history locked beneath downtown's busy streets. This book originated as a paper on just one of the sites we found, the remnants of a mid-twentieth-century African American–owned nightclub, which we presented at the annual meeting of the Society for Historical Archaeology in January 2006.

The University of Nevada Press approached us about expanding the paper into a book on the Harlem Club and its place within the larger context of race relations in Nevada. That was our intention when we began, but our conversations about Reno's historically diverse population kept leading us back to additional sites we had researched during the ReTRAC project. Again and again we found ourselves making connections between people as varied as the brothers who ran the Prohibition era bottling works on the west side of town and the prehistoric inhabitants of a village next to the Truckee River. We quickly concluded that many more of the ReTRAC sites deserved further exploration, and luckily the press agreed with us.

The process of using these diverse sites to explore the history of Reno in all its breadth and depth has been a challenging one, incorporating many different sources of information. We cannot provide an encyclopedic history of the Biggest Little City, but thanks to the investigation of the sites lying right beneath our feet, we can tell parts of Reno's story that have not yet been told. The sites, features, and artifacts discussed in this book reveal that the Reno area has been home to diverse, rich cultures for thousands of years.

Our primary goal is to present a few of the West's lesser-known stories, grounded in the history of a place we find particularly compelling.

This work builds on decades of research and study by others, and we thank them for their dedication to archaeology, history, and Nevada.

Many people contributed time and effort to this book and the complicated project from which it sprang, and it is impossible to thank them all enough. The City of Reno supported this research, and Mark Demuth of MADCON Consultation Services gave us the opportunity to work on ReTRAC. Thanks are due to our past and present colleagues from Western Cultural Resource Management, Inc. (WCRM), including Tom Lennon, Steve Mehls, Renee Kolvet, Lief Christian, and Bob Peterson. Much of our work was grounded in research done by Susan Stornetta, Tom Burke, Ron Reno, Vickie Clay, and C. Lynn Furnis in an earlier phase of the project. Don Hardesty and Eugene Hattori provided valuable guidance at several points along the way.

WCRM's intrepid archaeological monitors and field crews spent endless hours in all kinds of weather excavating sites and watching heavy equipment. Thank you. The Native American monitors on the Daylight site, Steve Nighthawk and Jeanne O'Day, faced some of the same challenges. Special thanks go to Jen Sigler for assistance well above and beyond what was required, and to Karen Laramore for her kind help with graphics and general morale.

We are grateful for the guidance of our agency contacts, including Ted Bendure at the Federal Highway Administration and Hal Turner at the Nevada Department of Transportation. Without the always timely assistance of Rebecca Palmer and Alice Baldrica at the Nevada State Historic Preservation Office in reviewing our many discoveries, the ReTRAC project would have never been completed.

Our research was immeasurably enriched by the help of our collaborators Oteria Cole, Onie Cooper, Wayne Crawford, Harold Curran, Dolores Feemster, Lonnie Feemster, Edward Folsom, Jean Hubbard, David Love, Darla Potter, and Norma Washington. Many of them reviewed chapters for us and helped us correct errors and omissions. Neal Cobb and Darla Potter provided additional help on general Reno history, and Michael Coray was kind enough to review portions of the manuscript as well. Michael Maher, Phillip Earl, Lee Brumbaugh, and Eric Moody of the Nevada Historical Society were ever helpful.

Many tribal members participated in consultation, but special thanks are due to Ben Aleck of the Pyramid Lake Paiute Tribe, William Dancing Feather and Linda Shoshone of the Washoe Tribe of Nevada and California, and Buck Sampson and Michon Ibn of the Reno-Sparks Indian Colony.

Matt Becker, Charlotte Dihoff, Sara Vélez Mallea, Kathleen Szawiola, and Joanne O'Hare at the University of Nevada Press guided us through the writing and revision process with endless patience. Thanks also to Melinda Conner for her copyediting skills, and to our anonymous peer reviewers for their help. Thanks are due to Robert Leavitt, Stephanie Livingston, D. Craig Young, Peter Wigand, Penny Rucks, Chuck Wheeler, Jaclyn Raley, and Bob Estes for all their work on the project.

And finally, thanks to the family and friends who supported us during the writing process, especially Eve and Steve Ringhoff, John Ringhoff, and Cheryl Stoner.

# The River and the Railroad

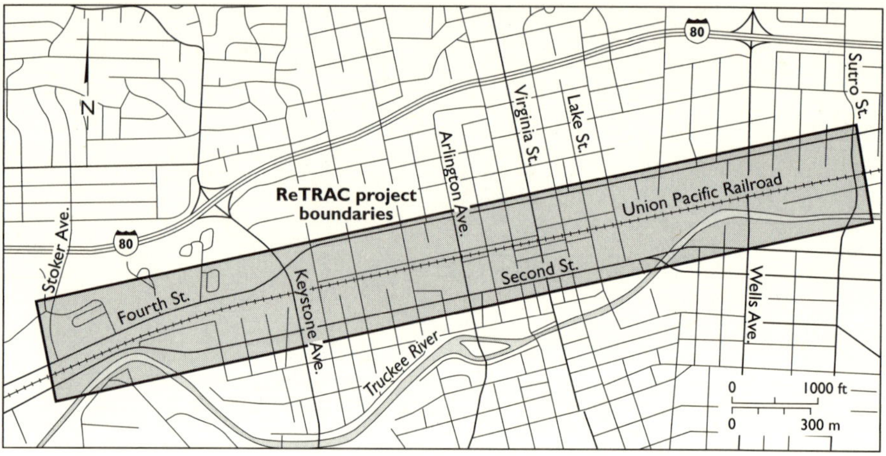


Reno and the ReTRAC project area.

# Introduction

The town that would become Reno sprang up between the Truckee River and the Central Pacific Railroad's transcontinental line in 1868. The main line railroad corridor has bisected the city ever since, sitting unchanged as Reno grew and evolved around it and posing obvious problems for traffic, public safety, and aesthetics. Over the years, city officials and residents proposed many solutions, including elevating the tracks, depressing them, and rerouting them, but the sheer magnitude of the undertaking made both residents and city government reluctant to act. The 1996 merger of the Union Pacific and Southern Pacific railroads precipitated a proposal by the city of Reno, Union Pacific, and the federal government to eliminate the existing railroad crossings in the central part of the city. After several years of political struggle, the proposal culminated in the Reno Transportation Rail Access Corridor (ReTRAC) project.

This undertaking, spanning 2001–05, involved the excavation of a large, partially covered trench in order to lower the railroad tracks through town over a length of more than two miles and a width of fifty-four feet. At its deepest point, the rail trench is thirty feet below the modern ground surface. Trains continue to run through Reno now, just underneath the day-to-day activities of the city.

The ReTRAC project was publicly funded and permitted, triggering mandatory protection of cultural resources.[1] Excavation and construction could not proceed without provisions for discovering, recording, and evaluating the significance of archaeological sites and their eligibility for listing in the National Register of Historic Places. Aboveground sites such as historical buildings also had to be recorded and protected. Through a subcontractor, the city of Reno hired Western Cultural Resource Management, Inc. (WCRM) to conduct archaeological and historical research for the ReTRAC project. This book reports some of the results of that research.

The ReTRAC project provided a rare opportunity to examine archaeological resources across a large area. Excavating the trench for the railroad tracks took a slice out of the center of town, in essence creating a cross-section of the oldest part of Reno. Related work including relocation of utilities, construction of grade crossings, and excavation of drainage channels took place outside the trench, further expanding the area exposed to archaeological examination. The preparation of a temporary "shoofly" track running along the entire south side of the proposed trench to enable transcontinental rail traffic to continue during trench construction exposed additional archaeological sites.

During the five years of the ReTRAC project, WCRM recorded eighty-three archaeological sites and one previously unrecorded basement room of a historic building: the 1873 Masonic Hall building at the corner of Sierra Street and Commercial Row. Two of the sites were prehistoric in age (predating written records) and eighty-one were historical. With the exception of the prehistoric Daylight site, most of the archaeological sites discovered during the course of the ReTRAC project had been damaged by previous modern activity; as a result, few had substantial or stratified artifact deposits. There were no privies, capped dumps, or other sites conducive to contextualized material preservation. We excavated in eight of the sites and conducted research with the help of Native American groups, local archival repositories, and local residents willing to share their knowledge and memories. The result was a great deal of new information about many different people of the past, starting as early as five thousand years ago and extending up into the late twentieth century.

As one of very few large-scale archaeological projects that have taken place in an urban setting in the western United States, the ReTRAC project was a rare opportunity to add to our understanding of Reno's prehistoric, historical, and modern inhabitants. The study also provided the chance to construct snapshots in time, exploring a shared heritage that transcends region, time period, culture, and topic. As Reno looks to its future, the stories uncovered during the course of our research can provide vital links to the city's past, engaging its diverse public in a continuing conversation about how this place was, is, and can be.

There are many ways to combine archaeological and historical information and use it to pursue specific research topics. Some approaches lean toward objective "scientific" inquiry, while others are more subjective and humanistic. This book employs a broad approach, sometimes referred to as "the archaeology of place," that is particularly conducive to combining data from archaeological and historical sources. Because it was restricted by the physical boundaries of the ReTRAC project, the archaeological research necessarily focused on the sites found within those boundaries. Most of the sites were downtown, and all were in or near the railroad corridor.

Our exploration of Reno's past is strongly rooted in the place itself—not just in the artifacts found, the date ranges derived from geochemical analyses, or any overarching archaeological theories. The landscape provides the backdrop against which to examine the countless individual activities that, woven together, make up a place.

The following chapters trace the growth of Reno in a roughly chronological manner from the earliest known occupations into the late twentieth century. Chapter 1 opens with a brief overview of Reno's development that provides background information on the prehistory and history of the area. Chapter 2 describes the Daylight site, a prehistoric village next to the Truckee River containing the stratified remnants of more than five thousand years of habitation. Research into this location has enabled an exploration of how people used the river's rich resources and adapted to ever-changing environments. Chapter 3 examines the role of railroad companies in the development of Reno's urban landscape and traces the evolution of that landscape into the present. Chapter 4 explores the laborious growth of Reno's infrastructure system as residents dealt with urban ditches, catastrophic fires, and "Reno chowder." Chapters 5 and 6 focus on two historical twentieth-century sites. Chapter 5 presents the history and archaeology of the Frank Brothers Bottling Works, a small business confronted first with national Prohibition and then with the Great Depression. Chapter 6 addresses the history and archaeology of several African American–owned clubs downtown, revealing tenacious responses to racial discrimination and segregation. The last chapter offers a few conclusions.

This book delves into just a few of the stories that have melded to make Reno the place that it is today. It presents Reno as a human landscape—one in which, as archaeologist Julian Thomas said, "personal biographies are built up from located acts."[2] The history of Reno includes habitual activities and unremarkable, day-to-day events as well as the larger triumphs and catastrophes usually preserved in writing and memory. Archaeology is a particularly useful way to learn the details about how people lived in the past. Such minutiae are not always dramatic, but they are more representative of reality than the more spectacular moments are. Reno's history contains many entertaining, often apocryphal legends. The city's story is sometimes poetic and lovely, but is just as often messy, complicated, and ugly. If we remember only the mythical tales about the Biggest Little City and forget the real lives—those often mundane, sometimes wonderful, occasionally terrible tales of the everyday—we do both the place and ourselves a disservice. Reno's truth lies somewhere in between the two extremes.

CHAPTER

1

# A Brief History of Reno

The first people to arrive in what would become Reno were not the fur trappers, surveyors, or emigrants of the 1840s, but hunter-gatherers who explored the valley thousands of years before that. At the western edge of the Great Basin, the river-fed, grassy valley that would later become known as the Truckee Meadows played host to migrating waterfowl, abundant animal life, and, probably, prehistoric people. Although no evidence for these early inhabitants has yet been discovered, the presence of Clovis points in Washoe Valley, about twenty miles to the south, indicates that people were probably in the Truckee Meadows by about 12,000 years ago.

Archaeologists divide prehistory into periods in order to compare prehistoric cultures from different eras. Interpretation and understanding of the cultural variability within the western Great Basin and Sierra Nevada is likewise informed by partitioning broad aspects of that variability into prehistoric components, or phases. Archaeologists Gordon Willey and Philip Phillips defined "phase" as "an archaeological unit possessing traits sufficiently characteristic to distinguish it from all other units similarly conceived, whether of the same or other cultures or civilizations, spatially limited to the order of magnitude of a locality or region and chronologically limited to a relatively brief interval of time."[1]

The time periods that units encompass are somewhat arbitrary and are constantly being revised as new information is discovered. They are also regionally dependent; the chronology for the Eastern Sierra Front, the area in which Reno is located, is different from chronologies in other parts of the Great Basin.

Archaeologists divide prehistory not only by phase, but also by adaptive strategy—what people did in a certain time period to adapt to changing environmental conditions. For the western Great Basin and the Eastern Sierra Front, these adaptive strategies fall into four periods: the Paleoarchaic, the Early Archaic, the Middle Archaic, and the Late Archaic.

*Chronology of the Eastern Sierra Front*

The date ranges below are based on calibrated radiocarbon years and are expressed as years before present (BP) or years ago for the sake of editorial simplicity.

*Climatic Periods and Geological Events*

| | |
|---|---|
| 10,500 | Pleistocene epoch and last ice age end and the Early Holocene begins; modern climates appear. |
| 10,500–7500 | Early Holocene: Climate warms and Pleistocene lakes such as pluvial Lake Lahontan diminish. |
| 7600 | Mount Mazama erupts, resulting in the Crater Lake caldera. Ash fall mantles much of the Great Basin. Volcanic ash washes from the slopes of Peavine Mountain and is redeposited on the Truckee River floodplain. |
| 7500–3500 | Middle Holocene: Global climate warms, resulting in droughts of varying length and intensity in the Great Basin. |
| 3500–present | Late Holocene: Climate becomes cooler and wetter with a gradual transition to modern climate. |
| 500–100 | Little Ice Age: Climate cools; alpine glaciers resurge. |
| 100–present | Climate becomes warmer and drier. |

*Cultural Periods and Phases*

| | |
|---|---|
| 10,000–8000 | Paleoarchaic period/Tahoe Reach phase: Peopling of the western Great Basin and Eastern Sierra Front; artifacts include large stemmed (Great Basin Stemmed) projectile points. |
| 8,000–4000 | Early Archaic period/Spooner phase: Artifacts include large side-notched and possibly Humboldt lanceolate projectile points. |
| 5000–3000 | Middle Archaic period/Early Martis phase: Artifacts include contracting stem points of the Elko-Martis series and Steamboat projectile points (dart points thrown using a spear thrower or atlatl), and large basalt bifaces. |

| | |
|---|---|
| 3000–1300 | Middle Archaic period/Late Martis phase: Artifacts include corner-notched and eared points of the Martis and Elko series; large basalt bifaces; and semisubterranean houses with internal storage pits. |
| 1300–700 | Late Archaic period/Early Kings Beach phase: Artifacts include Rosegate series projectile points (arrow tips); chert cores; bow and arrow technology; flakes and other small chert tools, and hullers utilized; house pits may be small, shallow, and saucer-shaped. |
| 700–150 | Late Archaic period/Late Kings Beach phase: Artifacts include Desert series projectile points; chert cores; flakes and other small chert tools utilized; house pits are shallow, saucer-shaped. |

The Paleoarchaic period in the Eastern Sierra Front occurred between 10,000 and 8,000 years ago and includes the Tahoe Reach phase of the eastern Sierra Nevada. The climate was becoming warmer and more arid then, and the great Pleistocene lakes were drying up. People presumably hunted big game as well as smaller animals, and consumed easily gathered and processed lake and marsh plants. Unlike the Archaic cultures to come, they did not grind seeds or live on sites long enough to accumulate midden or trash deposits; nor did they construct permanent structures or store resources.

The Early Archaic for the area is dated between 8,000 and 4,000 years ago and includes the Spooner phase. The warming trend continued during this period, and big game hunting remained a major focus of subsistence. The climate continued to warm and was characterized by droughts of varying length and intensity. People used grinding stones to process seeds, and used caves and rock shelters to store their goods and tools. Population numbers were low, and sites, including habitation areas, tended to be located on valley bottoms near permanent streams, but the uplands were also used.

The Middle Archaic spanned the time from 5,000 to 1,300 years ago and includes the Early and Late Martis phases of the eastern Sierra Nevada. The climate was cooler and moister than in the previous period, and Lake Tahoe overflowed its natural sill. Hunting had become more important, and hunters using atlatls (spear throwers) and dart points went out from base camps located on valley margins. People placed their base camps in areas with multiple resources, including hot springs and

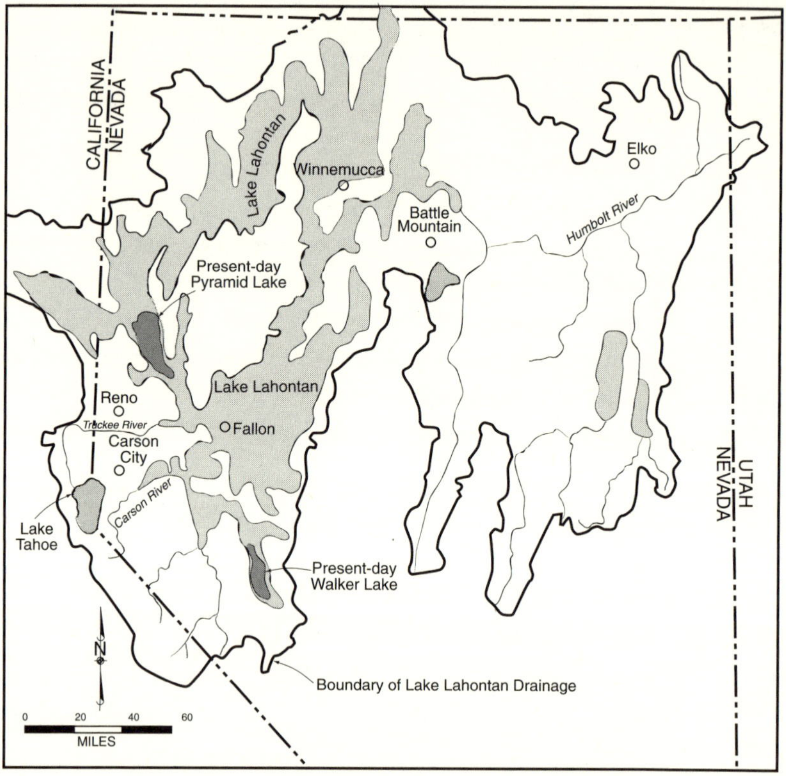


Northwestern Nevada and Lake Lahontan, ca. 15,000 BP.

tool stone sources. A number of known sites from this period contain substantial winter pit houses with hearths and cache pits.

Archaeologist Robert Elston proposed a basic Archaic settlement pattern for the Great Basin, with two alternate variations: a dispersed pattern and a restricted pattern.[2] The former was the typical pattern in the more arid regions of the western Great Basin subarea, which includes central Nevada; small residential groups frequently selected different winter and base camp sites from year to year to take full advantage of relatively unpredictable and scarce basic resources such as food and water. The restricted pattern prevailed throughout the Eastern Sierra Front, including the Truckee Meadows, between 4,000 and 2,000 years ago. At that time the climate was wetter and provided a resource base that was more reliable and abundant in relation to population density. In the Middle Archaic Martis phase, residential groups could regularly occupy optimally located sites, or "sweet spots," with easy access to a wide range of needed supplies. Thus, they could procure valuable resources such as large game at low cost, with few residential moves.[3]

The Late Archaic began about 1,300 years ago and lasted until shortly after contact with European Americans. The climate was drying again, and subsistence was based on seeds, fishing, and small game. The atlatl and dart were replaced by the bow and arrow, and flaked stone technology became more simplified. Houses became smaller and less complex and were built in shallow basins lacking internal cache pits.

The Kings Beach phase of the Late Archaic featured a more dispersed settlement pattern with less regular occupation of optimal sites.[4] This pattern was linked to a changing set of subsistence strategies characterized by people using progressively more diverse resources with greater intensity and exploiting a greater number of ecological zones. Groups continued to occupy the old sites but began also to occupy new sites in less optimal locations,[5] either because resources were being depleted faster at the old sites, necessitating more frequent moves, or because a growing population filled in the spaces between optimal locations.

The Truckee Meadows is located within traditional Washoe territory. In recent times the region was used by both Washoe and Northern Paiute groups. The Hokan-speaking Washoe lived primarily in valleys along the eastern Sierra slope and in the Lake Tahoe vicinity. Lake Tahoe is central to the Washoe territory, and groups from around the region spent summers there. The Washoe seasonal range extended as far north as Honey Lake Valley and as far south as Topaz Lake. The Washoe are believed to have occupied their present range for about five thousand years. Anthropologist Alfred Kroeber estimated the full strength of the tribe to have been approximately 1,500 at the time of contact in the early 1840s; the estimate was 900 in 1859.[6]

The Northern Paiute, or Paviotso, occupied a larger area estimated to cover a third of present-day Nevada as well as southeastern Oregon, southern Idaho, and eastern California.[7] Although not all researchers agree, linguistic evidence indicates the Numic-speaking Paiute entered the Great Basin approximately one thousand to two thousand years ago.[8]

Historical accounts allude to interactions between the two groups. Local writer Grace Dangberg noted that in 1863, Paiute and Washoe mixed in Antelope Valley (south of Gardnerville, about fifty miles south of Reno).[9] Frank Morgan, a Washoe consultant, reported confrontations between Washoe and Paiute Indians near McTarnahan Bridge, on the

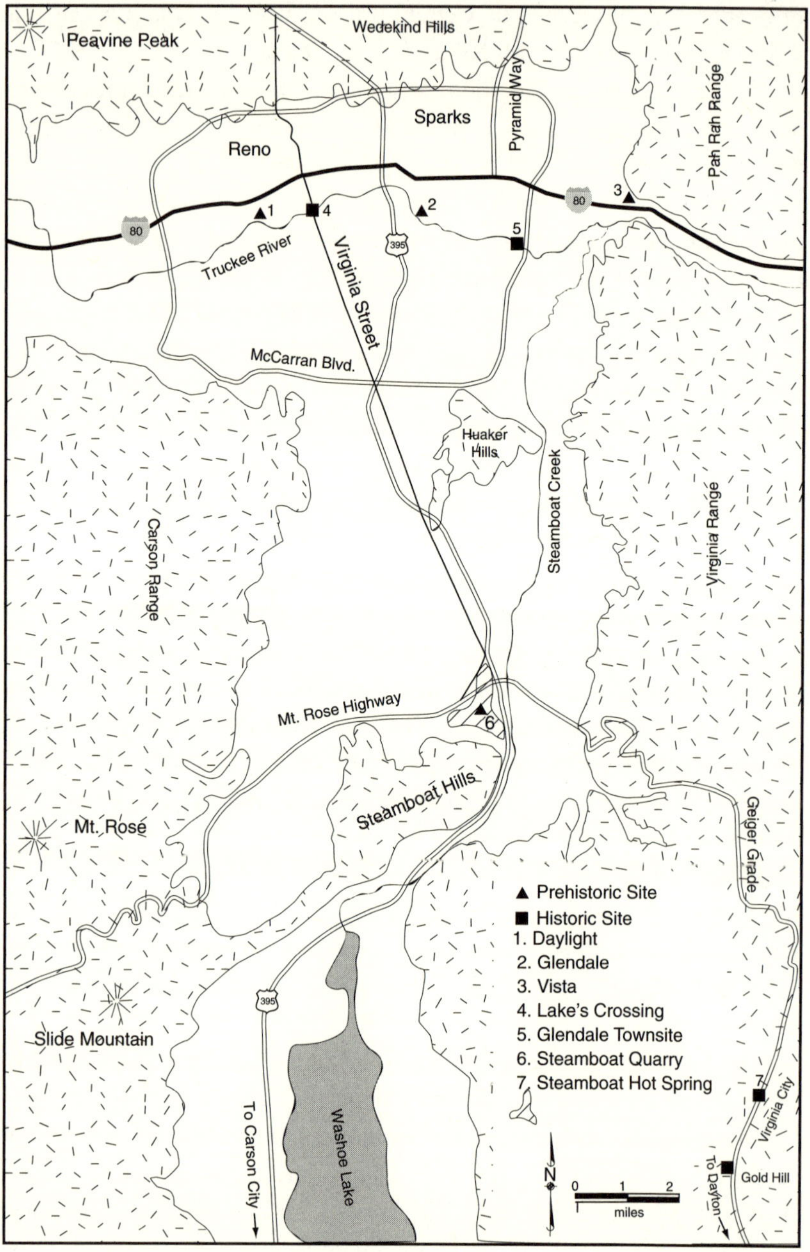


The Truckee Meadows, showing important prehistoric and historic locations.

East Fork of the Carson River south of Carson City.[10] This area, referred to as "Coyote Smokeout," was known for its abundant freshwater mussels and as a good source of quartz, and is the location of many Washoe legends. According to Dangberg, the Washoe were sometimes intimidated by their neighbors to the east; the Northern Paiute would not let them own horses, for example.[11]

Despite numerous accounts of friction, however, the two groups often had peaceable relations and intermarried. A Paiute consultant reported to ethnographer Willard Z. Park that the Washoe often traveled to Pyramid Lake in Paiute territory and were referred to as cousins.[12] In 1917 the federal government established the Reno-Sparks Indian Colony in a twenty-eight-acre tract that housed the Paiute tribe in the northern part and the Washoe in the south. A history of the Washoe tribe reports that the Numa and Washoe participated in intertribal hand games that offered social as well as competitive opportunities. One elderly Numa remembered them: "The Washo gamblers were mostly young men, and they would come over on the Paiute side of the colony to challenge the Paiute gamblers, who were mostly older women."[13]

Archaeologists studying Washoe sites have noted a low frequency of trade items such as obsidian from north and east of Washoe territory, but ample evidence of trade with Sierran and trans-Sierran groups.[14] The material record suggests more extensive trade between the Washoe and their southern and western (Sierran) neighbors than with the Northern Paiute.

In the vicinity of Reno, the Washoe once lived north of downtown near the future sites of the University of Nevada and the original Manogue High School campus, near Idlewild Park, and in several areas along the Truckee River.[15] In the Truckee Meadows, large archaeological sites have been located at Vista in eastern Sparks, Glendale, Huffaker Hills, the Mount Rose Fan, and near the sloughs in the former Double Diamond Ranch in the heart of the Truckee Meadows.

Fish was an important part of the diet of these groups, who used fishing platforms, dip nets, spears, and harpoons along the banks of Great Basin rivers.[16] Northern Paiute people living along the Truckee and Walker rivers set cone-shaped traps in willow weirs and placed minnow-catching basketry traps in shallow water. The 1852 diary of Mariett Foster Cummings provides a good description of Paiute line and hook fishing on the Truckee River in August: "They procured for me great numbers of little fish resembling a sardine which they caught with ingenious little hooks made of a little stick one fourth of an inch in length to which was fastened nearly at a right angle a little thorn. These were baited with the outside of an insect. The line was simply a linen thread with six of these hooks attached."[17]

Pine nuts were also an important staple for both the Washoe and Northern Paiute people. This nutritious resource was easily stored and was a mainstay during the winter months. In this region, pinyon pine trees grow only south of the Truckee and Humboldt rivers and east of the Sierra Nevada; near Reno, they grow in the Virginia Range. The Washoe, who were more closely tied to the resources of the Sierras, also relied on acorns and sometimes traded them. Although Pyramid Lake people gathered acorns south of Honey Lake, it is doubtful that they regularly consumed them.[18]

Pine nuts were more than just a nutritious meal; the pine nut harvest in the early fall was and is an integral part of the cultural and social lives of local groups.[19] Willard Z. Park's consultants reported that the Washoe usually harvested the west side of the Pinenut Mountains while the Paiute exploited the eastern slopes.[20] Hank Pete, a Washoe informant for anthropologists Stanley and Ruth Freed, noted that it was the task of one particular man to dream about pine nuts and pray that they would increase in number and not be full of worms.[21] Although he was not a shaman, this man had power and was the leader of the pine nut dance; he decided when the nuts were ready for picking. As part of the routine, a headman traveled to the hills to assess the crop and bring back samples. On his return, the group planned a "pow-wow" attended by the entire village at which they danced all night in a circle dance. During the ceremony, people tested the cones to determine when the harvest should begin; the crop was usually at its prime in early September. If a crop looked poor, the groups might dance for several nights to a full week before beginning the harvest.[22]

Rabbit drives, also in the fall, afforded ample opportunity for socializing as well as food procurement. The drives were organized by an elected "rabbit boss" who called everyone to a site on one end of a large flat area. The people drove rabbits—both jackrabbits and cottontails—into large nets that were reported to be thirty inches wide and up to three hundred feet long and killed the trapped prey with clubs or arrows. They used all parts of the animals: drying the meat or eating it fresh, cutting the fur into strips and weaving it into blankets, and cracking the bones open to retrieve the nutritious marrow. Plant resources such as grass seeds, roots, and berries were also crucial. Small and large mammals such as marmots, squirrels, deer, and pronghorn were consumed whenever possible. Cooperative driving of rabbits and pronghorn was common to both the Washoe and the Northern Paiute.

After European Americans settled in northern Nevada, the lifeways of the Paiute and Washoe changed dramatically. The newcomers destroyed pinyon forests for mining fuel and took over the most productive lands for agriculture, severely disrupting the lives of the aboriginal hunter-gatherers. The federal government established the first Indian reservation in western Nevada at Pyramid Lake in 1860 and created an Indian agency in Carson Valley for the Washoe people.[23] No land allotments were made for the Washoe until the late 1880s and early 1890s. The Dresslerville and Carson colonies were not established until the early twentieth century. Although they were among the first Native American groups in the Great Basin to experience the impact of the westward migration, the Washoe remained outside the influence of Indian agents, treaty commissions, and others who advocated reservations.[24] They continued to pursue traditional subsistence strategies, augmented by seasonal labor in lumber camps and mining towns, well into the twentieth century.[25]

Groups that did end up on reservations were encouraged by the government to farm. Those away from the reservations usually found work at farms or ranches, or worked for the railroads; the women worked as domestic servants. A small number of Paiutes worked as laborers on the Comstock. By 1870, most wore Western-style clothing and had abandoned many of their native traditions.[26] Between 1870 and 1929, the federal government's pan-reservation policy attempted to stamp out nativism. Northern Paiute and Washoe children were enrolled in government-run schools, such as the Stewart Indian School in Carson City, designed to turn children into rural farmers of Christian faith, and Indian communities into carbon copies of rural American towns.[27]

THE LUSH VALLEY that would become known as the Truckee Meadows was as attractive to the first European Americans to arrive in the region as it had been to native groups many years before. For overland emigrants exhausted from crossing one of the driest stretches of the trail west, the valley was a welcome resting place. It was the Elisha Stevens emigrant party from Council Bluffs, Iowa, that gave the name Truckee to the river in the Meadows. After crossing the Forty Mile Desert, the party had camped in the Humboldt Sink, northeast of the Truckee Meadows, and debated whether to finish the trek to California so late in the season. A Paiute man had approached the group, intending to trade, and dropped his robe to show them he was unarmed and meant them no harm. The emigrants interpreted his name as "Truckee." The man offered to guide them to a river located a few days' travel to the west that would lead them straight to the Sierra Nevada. They reached the river near present-day Wadsworth on 9 October 1844, and followed it to become the first known emigrant group to pass through the Truckee Meadows. Thankful for the assistance of its guide, the party named the river after him. Although the river had already been named the Salmon Trout River by John C. Frémont earlier that year, Truckee was the name that stuck.

Author Edwin Bryant described the Truckee Meadows as they appeared in 1846:

> About 12 o'clock we emerged from the confined limits between the high ranges of mountains, affording us, in many places, room barely sufficient to pass, without leaving the bottom of the river, into a spacious and highly fertile valley, eight or ten miles in diameter. The grasses in this valley are very luxuriant, and their varieties numerous. There is no timber, with the exception of the clumps of small willows belting the stream, and fringing the margin of a deep and miry slough, which runs entirely across it. Pine timber, however, of stately dimensions, begins to exhibit itself on the sides and summits of the surrounding mountains. In crossing the valley on the southern side, we passed through several miles of tule, a species of rush, or reed, which here grows to the height of eight feet, on the wet or swampy soil. We saw numbers of deer and antelope in the valley, and I noticed in several places fresh footprints of a horse.[28]

The infamous Donner Party passed through the Truckee Meadows in October 1846, several months after Edwin Bryant's party. The group's well-known fate in the Sierras that winter may have discouraged some others from using that route to California over the Sierra Nevada, but the valley continued to see an influx of emigrants every summer. Emigrant traffic became much heavier after gold was discovered in California in 1848. By the 1850s the Truckee Meadows had become a well-known overland stop on the way to California on the Stevens-Donner route, also known as the Truckee-Donner route.

Local entrepreneurs began providing services for the emigrants along this trail. H. H. Jamison built his ranch and trading post, called Jamison's Station, on the Truckee River in 1852 and may have been the first European American to winter in the valley. Charles Gates and John Stone established Stone and Gates' Crossing at Glendale in 1857, boasting a free bridge and a trading post; their crossing became the most popular. European American settlement of the area remained sparse at first. Historian John M. Townley noted that in 1858 the Truckee Meadows had only about twenty-five full-time residents, most of them ranchers.[29] The Native American population of the valley at this time is unknown. It would have been primarily Washoe and Paiute, many of whom had been involuntarily displaced from their traditional lands by ranches and settlements.

The 1859 discovery of gold at what would become known as Gold Hill and the subsequent Ophir strike brought an influx of people and capital pursuing the riches of the Comstock Lode. Virginia City boomed, and things began to change in the Truckee Meadows. The 1860 federal census counted 105 residents in the Truckee Meadows, only 8 of whom were female; occupations listed included merchant, laborer, teamster, and rancher.[30] As usual, Native Americans were not counted by census-takers, so the Washoe and Paiute populations of the Truckee Meadows in 1860 are not known. Charles W. Fuller built a toll bridge over the Truckee sometime between 1859 and 1860, and its use increased along with the traffic to the booming Comstock. In 1861 workers completed a road connecting the Truckee River to Virginia City; it eventually extended into the Sierras and was used by traffic on the Henness Pass/Donner Lake route. After Myron C. Lake bought the bridge and toll franchise from Fuller in 1861, it became known as Lake's Crossing. Lake also built a hotel called Lake House. When flooding destroyed all of the area's bridges, Lake hastened to rebuild his bridge first. He added a livery stable, a blacksmith shop, a brick kiln, and a water-powered grist mill, and acquired an exclusive ten-year franchise on his toll road.[31] Before long, Lake's Crossing was a well-known stop for stagecoaches connecting Virginia City and the Comstock with other parts of northwestern Nevada and northeastern California. Lake's Crossing was located near the present-day Truckee River Bridge on Virginia Street, on the future site of the Riverside Hotel.

In 1862 President Abraham Lincoln convinced Congress to pass the first Pacific Railroad Act, which chartered the Union Pacific Railroad, recognized California's Central Pacific Railroad, and authorized those companies to build the transcontinental railroad route. As Central Pacific engineers and surveyors examined possible routes, they recognized the need for a station in the Truckee Meadows to serve the Comstock market and to be the interchange point with future local rail lines. Among the latter would be the Virginia & Truckee Railroad, constructed in 1869. The land near modern Glendale, a few miles east of Lake's Crossing, was a strong candidate for the station; it was comparatively flat, but it was also prone to spring flooding. A timely flood convinced the rail builders that higher ground such as that at Lake's Crossing would be a better location for the new rail line. Lake sold the railroad about 160 acres for the townsite that would support the station. Central Pacific first called the town Argenta but changed the name to Reno two weeks later, in honor of Union general Jesse Lee Reno, and set about platting the townsite. The railroad began auctioning off lots on 9 May 1868. The first train arrived in the new community in June, and Reno's position as a hub of freight for the Comstock was assured.

In addition to bringing one hundred or so railroad employees to town, the railroad also spawned warehousing and transfer companies, hotels and other commercial houses, and support businesses. The railroad depot gave the new community a focal point, and a distinctive commercial area developed around the street on which it faced, Commercial Row. A wide variety of businesses flourished along Commercial Row, which became the center of Reno during the late nineteenth century. Rail interchange traffic developed rapidly, first with the Virginia & Truckee, and later with the Nevada-California-Oregon Railway Company.

During the summer of 1868 an unidentified young reporter for the *San Francisco Times* traveled the existing length of the Central Pacific railroad line, reporting his experiences along the way. His description of Reno reveals a vibrant, if uncouth, young town:

> Reno is situated in the middle of a frightful plain, destitute of any feature of beauty or picturesqueness. It is one of those mushroom towns that seem to spring up in a single night, like Aladdin's Palace, and from the nature of its elements its sudden evanishment would be scarcely matter for surprise . . . people rush into Reno and gobble up whatever fuel in the shape of meals they can get; and never grumble, and drink bad whisky without a murmur; and doze on chairs, or make their bones ache by lying on boards, and rush away again, by rail or stage, and Reno cares nothing, but swelters on in the broiling sun, while all the day the sharp tapping of hammers and grating of saws accompanies the erection of new buildings and all the night the fiddles go, and the glasses clink, and the general hurry and bustle is brought to a climax now and then by a lively shooting affray. . . . Busy Reno has no concern with the fate, present, past or future, of any one of her motley population. She is on the railroad, and has a "big thing"; and she is bent upon making her pile with what speed she can command; and the pace of Reno is by no means contemptible.[32]

Nascent Reno did not seem to be a place destined for long-term prosperity. Although it had the security of location along the railroad's main line, that was no guarantee of longevity. For its first decade the community was almost totally dependent on the vagaries of the Comstock. If there was anything consistent about nineteenth-century mining booms, it was the fact that they were followed by busts. As a backup, Reno had the beef and grain produced by ranchers and farmers in the Truckee Meadows and shipped to both Virginia City and San Francisco. But the fertile valley is relatively small and vulnerable to sudden climate-caused drops in productivity, as illustrated by the harsh winter of 1890 and Nevada's frequent droughts. The little community paid no mind. Entrenched in the frontier mindset of exploiting as much as possible as quickly as possible, Reno's residents worked hard to make as much money as they could before it was too late. "For over a decade," noted Townley, "Reno stayed an overcrowded, underbuilt, busy, undistinguished 'railroad' town with little excuse for being other than shipping beef to California and supplying the Comstock with its fifty carloads of necessaries every day via the V&T."[33]

Reno resident Bertha Bender Brown, born in Reno in 1877, recalled the sound of the trains running through town:

> Being only a block from the tracks, we would hear, every night, the deep roaring and chugging of the giant engines as they gathered their flocks of box cars to pull up over the steep grades to Truckee and beyond over the Donner Summit in the high Sierras. The clicking of the wheels on the rails, the shudder and crash as two sections were locked together, the long-drawn whistles, so much sharper on cold nights, and then the solid roaring as the engines gathered head and steam for the long steep haul, these are the remembered music of my girlhood.[34]

Reno kept going and established itself at a rapid pace, with residential areas growing up around the downtown commercial core and a few impressive permanent commercial buildings appearing. The Masonic Hall, completed in 1873 at the corner of Commercial Row and Second Street, was one of Reno's first masonry buildings and still stands today. So does the Odd Fellows' Hall, built in 1877 at the corner of Second and Virginia. Banks and every kind of commercial enterprise opened downtown.

From its beginning, Reno's population was composed of a wide variety of ethnic groups ranging from native Washoe and Northern Paiute to Basque, Chinese, Arabian, South African, and Chilean. The 1910 federal census noted more than thirty nationalities.[35] By 1920, India, Turkey, the Philippines, Syria, Korea, Japan, Brazil, and Italy were represented as well.[36] Non-native-born people owned many of the businesses on Commercial Row. The 1920 census recorded entrepreneurs from Poland, Germany, Syria, Russia, Armenia, Persia, Turkey, Romania, Greece, China, and Italy doing business there.[37] As Reno developed, some of its eth-

The Masonic Hall (on the corner, to the right of the Wieland's Beer sign) and other Commercial Row buildings, ca. 1906. Courtesy of the Nevada Historical Society.

nic groups began to self-segregate into neighborhoods. Little Italy, for instance, located generally along Lake Street between First Street and Commercial Row, was well known as the commercial center for both immigrant Italians and their native-born descendants. The town had another, even more prominent Little Italy on the west side, but this area was residential rather than commercial. Many of Reno's Italians were the stonemasons and bricklayers who gave some of the early residential and commercial buildings their distinctive architectural character. Reno's Chinatown, located along First Street between Virginia and Lake streets, was established even earlier. The presence of many different cultural groups is typical of urban centers in the West. Mining towns such as Virginia City had diverse populations drawn by the prospect of riches, and it follows that a distribution center such as Reno would attract people of all types for the same reason.

Reno's early infrastructure developed in direct response to problems that emerged as the city grew. The most notorious problem began as soon as the town was founded in 1868: the community suffered a series of fires that caused varying degrees of destruction over the next two decades. This, too, was typical of western towns, which initially relied on wood construction, had many structures built close together, and rarely invested in centralized fire protection precautions until inspired to do so by one or more catastrophic conflagrations. After weathering several smaller fires, Reno faced its first major inferno in October 1873 when a blaze started in the Western Hotel and spread to neighboring blocks, destroying about 100 buildings along Commercial Row. In 1877 the topmost story of the three-story Depot Hotel went up in flames, killing chambermaid Lena Johnson. The most destructive fire occurred on 2 March 1879, when strong winds spread sparks from a building's chimney to a stack of firewood, then fanned the flames to adjoining buildings. The ensuing firestorm destroyed about 350 buildings, consuming brick and masonry structures as well as wooden ones, and killed six people.[38] It remained the deadliest fire in Reno's history until 1962, when the Golden Hotel fire killed six people; and 2006, when the Mizpah Hotel fire claimed twelve lives.

The fires were but one of the urbanization problems Reno faced as its population grew. Soon the community suffered from water supply and water quality problems that prompted municipal involvement and resulted in the establishment of water companies. The burgeoning town also needed to deal with sewage; the open ditches and even the swiftly flowing Truckee River showed the ill effects of years of indiscriminate sewage discharge. Finally, provisions for utilities such as electricity, telephone service, and gas had to be made. Because the railroad was in the center of town, many of these issues first became obvious along the tracks, and the first attempts to solve them also took place there. During the late nineteenth century and continuing to the present, the streets and the rail corridor became routes for water lines, gas lines, electrical conduits, storm and domestic sewer lines, and other pipelines.[39]

The rapid growth of the European American population did direct damage to the Truckee River's natural riparian habitat and changed the face of the entire valley. Sawmills upstream from Reno discharged sawdust directly into the river; this clouded the water, killed off fish, and even created a man-made delta of sawdust at Pyramid Lake. Added to the sawdust was a noxious mix of the lubricants used to float logs down flumes into the river; tallow, dogfish oil, and rancid butter were common ingredients. In the winter of 1879 the Truckee River was said to look like melted butter as it flowed under the Virginia Street Bridge in downtown Reno.[40] Lumber companies also built diversion dams such as the large one in Verdi, which redirected almost the entire flow of the river through a large holding pond for retaining the logs flowing downstream.[41] In addition to lowering the river's water quality to undrinkable standards, these industrial activities significantly damaged native fish populations. The sewage discharged directly into the river contributed to the decline in water quality, including spurring the growth of algae where none had been seen before. At times of low flow in the summer, effluvia piled up on the banks of the river, sometimes for months before the water level rose enough to wash the foul mess downstream. Increased agriculture-related irrigation activity in the 1870s led to more water diversion and further changes to the natural environment with the establishment of large fields of alfalfa and other crops.

Its steady growth, diversifying economy, and close ties to the capital-rich urban centers of San Francisco and Sacramento helped Reno weather the slow decline of the Comstock during the 1880s without too much hardship. The University of Nevada moved from Elko to Reno in 1887, establishing Reno as the educational and cultural center of Nevada. The town also successfully advertised itself as a vacation destination ideal for both recreation and health, touting its clean, dry air as the perfect environment for consumptives and invalids.[42] Growth was slow but constant: Reno went from a little over 1,000 people in 1880 to 3,500 in 1890 and 4,500 in 1900, even as Nevada lost almost 35 percent of its population in a statewide depression.[43]

By the 1890s the town was still fairly rural, closely tied to transportation and cattle ranching, and adjusting to the decline of the mining-based economy. Historian William Rowley described Reno and Nevada in this period as "fixed in old frontier time and social attitudes. One result was that laws did not change at the rate they did in other states. By the time the 20th century arrived the state and its communities were in some respects outdated and even [had] anachronisms. But in this arrested development . . . the city and the state would find much of their 20th-century identity."[44]

The first two decades of the twentieth century saw an important shift in the local economy that would bring the town national significance: a focus on recreation, motivated by those who came to Reno for expedient divorces. Nevada's divorce law, which had a six-month residency requirement, had remained largely unchanged since it was adopted in 1861 while most other states instituted more stringent divorce laws, including residency requirements of at least one year. In 1906 Laura Corey, the wife of U.S. Steel president William E. Corey, came to Reno for a divorce. Her case was highly publicized in the newspapers and attracted attention to Reno as a haven for those seeking marital dissolution. By 1910 the town's reputation was well known, and many a wealthy divorce-seeker came to stay at the hotels, apartments, and dude ranches that sprang up to serve the needs of this new temporary population.[45] Not everyone in Nevada was comfortable with Reno's newfound reputation as the divorce capital of America, and in 1913 the state legislature successfully lengthened the divorce residency requirement from six months to one year. Reno's business community marshaled its forces, and in 1915 the legislature restored the original six-month residency requirement.

In the crucial period of the 1920s, Reno faced a choice: adopt stricter regulations on drinking, gambling, and prostitution, or keep access to these vices open and unrestricted in the interest of profit and growth. The nationwide Progressive reform movement resulted in many states outlawing the three vices, and Nevada was drifting toward some of the same changes. However, Reno did not embrace moral reform quite as thoroughly as some other cities; after all, as Rowley noted,

> a sparkling pure city simply was not good business for this mountain and desert center that entertained miners and cowboys and promoted a flourishing divorce industry. Reno . . . stood at a difficult crossroads in its history. It had been the focal point of urban growth in the state for the past 20 years and also of the state's weak Progressive reform movement. Reform in Reno as in Nevada had experienced rough sledding. Gambling had been curtailed, not abolished; divorce, prostitution, and drinking survived to taunt the reformers. Statewide prohibition had been accepted only at the last minute under the pressure of wartime necessity in 1918.[46]

In the mayoral election of 1923, the two visions of Reno's future went head-to-head. On one side, the moral reformers and their candidate, Mayor H. E. Stewart, argued that Reno was headed for ruin unless it abandoned seedy practices like allowing the red-light district to flourish. On the other side were the "unreformed" and their candidate, E. E. Roberts, who argued that Reno should remain wide open for both economic and ethical reasons. Roberts won in a landslide and went on to win two more terms in office.

When the state legislature reduced the divorce residency requirement to three months in 1927, Nevada reaped additional benefits from other states' strict reform laws. Likewise, when California instituted the "three-day gin marriage law," a three-day waiting period, couples in a hurry started traveling to Reno for their nuptials. In 1931, in response to competition from several other states, Nevada reduced the divorce residency requirement to a mere six weeks.

Nevada's best-known characteristic, legal gambling, survived a strict antigambling law that took effect on 1 October 1910. In 1915 the laws were relaxed to allow games of skill such as poker and faro; only games of chance such as roulette and slot machines remained illegal. In 1931 the state once again permitted gambling of all kinds. The state made the production and sale of alcohol illegal in 1918, two years before national Prohibition, but that did little to curb drinking in Reno (see chapter 5).

Reformers attacked prostitution as another of Reno's vices, but it remained legal until the 1940s. The city shut down the downtown red-light "restricted district," which was located along First Street near the river, for a brief period during World War I but reopened it immediately afterward.

Reno pursued another lucrative enterprise around the turn of the century: hosting prizefights. These events drew large crowds and reaped great profits. The best known was the 1910 "Fight of the Century" between Jack Johnson and Jim Jeffries, which drew a crowd of more than 30,000 and was the highest-profile event to have taken place in Reno up to that time. Johnson, the charismatic African American world champion heavyweight, handily beat Jeffries, who had come out of retirement to fight as America's "Great White Hope." Johnson's victory effectively silenced critics who thought a black man did not deserve to be the heavyweight champion of the world. All eyes were on Reno that day, and the city basked in the attention. "The world was starting to notice Reno," Rowley noted, "—a wild, raucous town in a beautiful mountainous setting where divorce seekers, cowboys, free-flowing liquor, and boxing fans mingled openly in a wide-open society."[47]

Like other American towns, Reno suffered economic hardship during the Great Depression after the 1929 stock market crash. Even though all forms of gambling were relegalized in 1931, Reno's card rooms kept a low profile in downtown alleys, trying not to draw too much attention for fear of reinvigorating antigambling crusaders. Gambling provided an important safety net for the local economy through the tax revenues and license fees it generated. Divorce remained an important industry as well, and such New Deal programs as the Civilian Conservation Corps and the Works Progress Administration boosted the local economy during those tough times.

Reno entered a new phase of growth after the Depression. Spurred by the establishment of larger, more prominent gambling operations that moved games of chance from the back alleys to Virginia Street, tourist traffic increased and Reno's image as a dingily glamorous place grew even stronger. In his 1941 book *Reno,* journalist Max Miller described what it was like to enter town for the first time:

> When the train stops at Reno, one knows he has stopped at Reno, and none other. He does not have to ask the conductor: "What town is this?" For Reno throws its worst face directly at the station, and appears to take pleasure in doing so, appears to take pleasure in indicating a turmoil of shack-stores, cheap

saloons, a burleycue of gambling houses, even a tattoo shop, tough alleys—and a blur of constant excitement. This is the way it seems when one gets off the train.[48]

After World War II, large casinos such as Harold's Club and Harrah's came to dominate downtown and opened up new recreational opportunities for locals and tourists. These opportunities were not open to everyone, though; African Americans were not allowed in most downtown casinos and restaurants (see chapter 6). In 1947 Reno restricted casino gambling to a commercial district centered on Virginia Street, with a "red line" drawn around it. The boundaries of the district were contested, most tenaciously by casino entrepreneur Ernie Primm, who pushed throughout the 1950s for expansion beyond the red line limits. Primm eventually succeeded in opening a new hotel on the west side of Virginia Street, outside the red line, in which gaming was "incidental."[49] In 1961 Primm announced plans to expand his Primadonna Club and promoted a heavily circulated petition to allow gambling on North Sierra Street. The petition garnered the signatures of almost two-thirds of Reno's voters,[50] and the city council gave in. Other casinos followed. In the late 1960s Nevada's gambling laws were changed to allow out-of-state corporations to enter the state gambling business. Over the next thirty years this would lead to significant changes in the essential nature of Reno's commercial district: near-total out-of-state corporate ownership of downtown casinos. In 1970 the city completely removed the Red Line Ordinance.

The Reno area became even more tourist oriented over the rest of the twentieth century as large hotel-casinos replaced many of the older businesses. Beginning with the 1960 Winter Olympics at Squaw Valley, the city also worked to position itself as a mecca for outdoor recreation. By this time the once-verdant Truckee River corridor looked nothing like it had just one hundred years earlier. Extensive flood control activities in the 1950s had eliminated most of the river's natural meanders and islands, and deepened and straightened the river channel. The native Pyramid Lake cutthroat trout became extinct sometime between 1938 and 1944, the victim of blocked spawning runs, overfishing, and pollution. The Nevada Division of Water Resources noted that it "took less than one hundred years to completely decimate this once plentiful species."[51]

Souvenir stores and pawn shops preying on out-of-town gamblers slowly replaced downtown businesses, and the large department stores that had flourished downtown during the 1940s and 1950s began moving to the outskirts of the city. Commercial Row, while certainly affected by the growth of large gambling establishments downtown, did not itself succumb to casino construction until the 1970s and 1980s. The expansion of Harrah's and the construction of Fitzgerald's Hotel and Casino and its associated parking structure completed the street's transformation. No longer the heart of Reno, Commercial Row had become a semi-accessible street useful only for reaching a few large casinos.

By the 1980s and 1990s Reno's downtown had become an anomaly—its largest businesses, the casinos and hotels, were largely owned by out-of-state corporations instead of locals. Most of the historical downtown buildings had been demolished to make way for new high-rises. Reno residents avoided the central business district, especially after the construction of interstate highways that bypassed downtown. Numerous revitalization projects were proposed, including a depressed trench for the railroad tracks, but none was instituted. The local populace was justifiably suspicious of such proposals, seeing them as benefiting the downtown casino owners but not ordinary Reno residents.[52]

Union Pacific still had an active railroad line carrying freight trains through the center of town every day, however, finally prompting the largest municipal project ever undertaken in Reno. The ReTRAC project, which created perhaps the biggest change yet to downtown Reno, represented the collaboration and compromise of many different parties. Its history is fraught with political intrigue and open conflict between and among residents and city government. The fortunes of the railroad and downtown Reno are nowhere else so obviously intertwined as in this project. For the first time in Reno's history, the day-to-day activities of downtown residents, workers, and visitors would not be affected by train traffic.

CHAPTER

2

# Occupants of the Daylight Site

No one knows who the first people that entered the Truckee Meadows were, or from where they came. The names they gave to the area's mountains and hills, valley, and river will likewise never be known. But the physical traces of early inhabitants of the Truckee Meadows, though rare, are undeniably present.

The stream these early people encountered, later known as the Truckee River, was once much larger than it is today. During the Late Pleistocene epoch, between 126,000 and 10,000 years ago, ice age glaciers in the Sierra Nevada influenced the flow and course of the river. A large glacier extending from Squaw Valley blocked the Truckee and raised the level of Lake Tahoe by almost thirty feet above its present height. This is apparent in the form of shoreline terraces that are visible at an elevation well above the modern lake. As the glaciers thinned and retreated at the end of the Pleistocene, the Squaw Valley glacier broke under the weight of the impounded lake. The resulting catastrophic floods carved the Truckee River canyon to the west of Reno and transported a tremendous volume of water and sediment, including numerous large boulders, into the Truckee Meadows and beyond. The Squaw Valley flood likely inundated a large part of the Meadows as it drained into the lower Truckee Canyon, past present-day Sparks.

High river flows, though much reduced from the earlier climactic floods, continued as precipitation and glacial melting raised the levels of Lake Lahontan. Fifteen thousand years ago this gigantic lake covered more than 8,500 square miles of northwestern Nevada and even parts of northeastern California.[1] The stream flow was well above the modern average for much of the Late Pleistocene and into the Early Holocene, which dates between 10,000 and 8,000 years ago, and created a deeply incised river channel. As it entered the Truckee Meadows, the Early Holocene river began to alter the flood-carved Pleistocene channel in the central portion of the valley, where modern downtown Reno is now located. The meandering river built a series of bars, levees, and sand-filled channels with sediment left behind by Late Pleistocene floods and flows, ranging from fine sands to large boulders. By the beginning of the Middle Holocene, around 8,000 years ago, the Truckee River stream flow ebbed as drought conditions prevailed. The modern floodplain had yet to develop, and abandoned gravel swales—small topographic depressions, channels, and levees—dominated the landscape.

Beginning about 5,400 years ago, the extreme drought of the Middle Holocene came to an end; by 4,500 years ago, relatively wet conditions had returned, along with seasonal flooding.[2] In the Truckee Meadows, floodplains built as the river overtopped its shallowly entrenched Middle Holocene channel and associated meander bars to deposit fine silts and sands. The floodplains gradually buried early Holocene landforms such as levees on the channel margins. These overbank floods were generally short-term events; the floodplain was dry most of the time and open for colonization by plants, animals, and people. At one of these old levees, just north of the Truckee and west of the location of modern downtown Reno, conditions were just right for the deposition of four distinct overbank/floodplain strata, or layers. Each of these layers contains evidence of human occupation, evoking images of many generations living in this place next to the river.

These are the layers that compose the Daylight site, a rare place containing evidence of more than 5,000 years of human activity. The site lay untouched beneath the Central Pacific Railroad tracks for 136 years until it was discovered in 2004. Its name comes from its location at the western end of the train trench, where the trains emerge, or "daylight," from the trench up onto the surface. The total size of the site is unknown because archaeological investigations were restricted to the trench corridor. Based on the excavation of the site, however, we do know that the site extends to the north at least as far as West Fourth Street and to the south toward the river, and is likely intact.

Archaeological monitors discovered the site during backhoe removal of the historical railroad bed, which was built up from fill material that included rock from other locations. In the process of removing the old railroad bed fill, the backhoe cut into the previously undisturbed surface of the site. The profile created by the backhoe cut contained stone artifacts, bone, charcoal, and burned rocks. Railroad bed removal stopped, and excavation of the site began. Archaeologists ultimately excavated 90 square meters (about 970 square feet) by hand, along with several backhoe trenches and auger test probes. The excavation spanned May–November 2004.

The Daylight site is a rare type in the Truckee Meadows for two reasons: it is stratified, and it is open. That is, the site contains intact layers representing multiple human occupations, and it is not in a rock shelter or other covered context. The processes of soil deposition and erosion in the Truckee Meadows are such that intact open, stratified sites are uncommon—or are presumed to be so. The survival of the Daylight site suggests that stratified open sites may not be as rare in the Truckee Meadows as was previously assumed.

Archaeologists use two main types of dating techniques: relative and absolute. Stratigraphy is the single best way of determining the relative ages of archaeological materials. The Law of Superposition states that the stratum (layer) that is younger will be on top of the strata that are older, given normal conditions of deposition. Cultural materials within each of the layers then follow the same sequence. In much of the Great Basin there is a stratigraphic feature that is useful in dating sites. Mount Mazama in Oregon erupted approximately 7,600 years ago, covering a large geographic area, including much of northern Nevada, with ash. This volcanic ash, or tephra, is a "marker horizon": everything found above it is known to be less than 7,600 years old, and everything found below it is more than 7,600 years old.

Another relative dating technique uses distinctive projectile point types that date to certain time periods. Steamboat points were the oldest type at the Daylight site, and were found with Early Martis features and deposits. Elko points were associated with Late Martis deposits, and Rosegate points with Early Kings Beach features and deposits. Desert Series points were found with the Late Kings Beach deposits.

Absolute dating techniques include radiocarbon dating—a radiometric dating method that uses the naturally occurring radioactive isotope carbon-14 (14C) to determine the age of organic materials up to about 60,000 years old. Raw, uncalibrated radiocarbon ages are usually reported in radiocarbon years before present (BP), with "present" being defined as AD 1950. Radiocarbon ages in years BP are almost always expressed as time ranges rather than precise years. Such raw dates can be calibrated to give calendar dates, which are generally expressed using the traditional acronyms BC (before Christ) and AD (anno Domini, a Latin term meaning "in the year of our Lord"). For example, if one is describing an event that occurred in the Late Pleistocene, some 12,000 years ago, and present is defined as AD 1950, 1,950 years are subtracted from 12,000, giving the year 10,050 BC. Other absolute dating techniques include such things like obsidian hydration dating.[3]

When discussing the layers of a stratified site, archaeologists begin at the bottom, or earliest, layer and work their way up to the most recent. As noted in chapter 1, local sequences of events are discussed in terms of phases that have both chronological (time-sensitive) and spatial elements. Based on projectile point types, radiocarbon dates, and climate, researchers have defined six chronological phases for the Eastern Sierra Front.[4] This geographical area stretches from Honey Lake Valley in the north to Antelope Valley in the south, and from the crest of the Sierra Nevada in the west to the Pah Rah, Virginia, and Pine Nut ranges in the east. The six chronological phases are, from oldest to youngest:

Tahoe Reach: 10,000–8,000 years BP
Spooner: 8,000–5,000 years BP
Early Martis: 5,000–3,000 years BP
Late Martis: 3,000–1,300 years BP
Early Kings Beach: 1,300–700 years BP
Late Kings Beach: 700–150 years BP

There is little evidence for human occupation of the Truckee Meadows during the Tahoe Reach phase. Evidence for the Tahoe Reach phase in the area consists of small sites, most located along the upper reaches of the Truckee River below Lake Tahoe, that contain large stemmed projectile points. During the Tahoe Reach phase the climate was warming and the pluvial lakes such as Lahontan had all but disappeared. The Daylight site did not contain any archaeological deposits dating to this time period.

With the exception of the Daylight site, the Truckee Meadows exhibits little evidence for the Spooner phase.[5] The Daylight site contained deposits dating to the end of the Spooner phase; this layer of sediment was

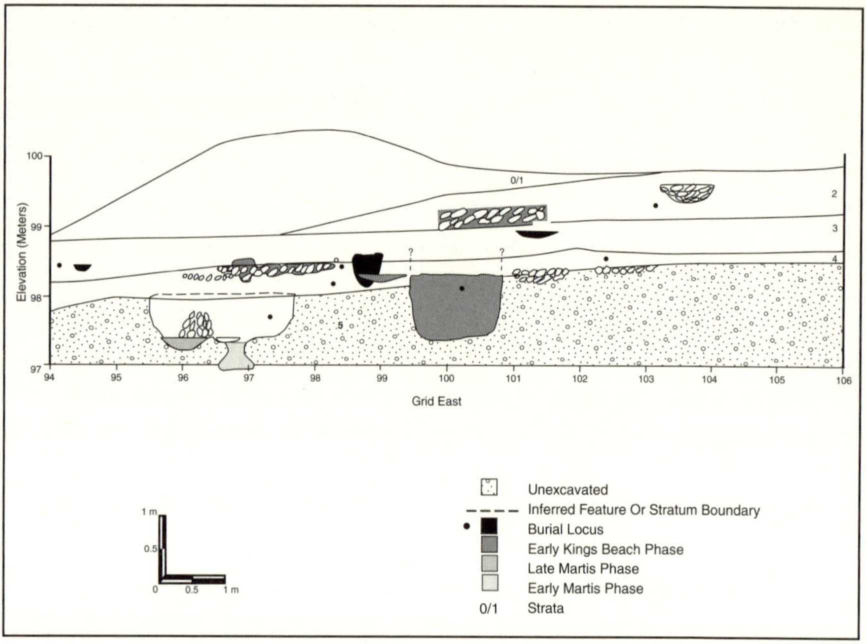


Stratigraphic cross section from the Daylight site, and the chronological phases associated with each stratum. Courtesy of WCRM, Inc.

Stratum 5, and it was the oldest and deepest stratum found at the site. The four later chronological phases are commonly found in the Truckee Meadows, and the Daylight site was no exception; researchers found deposits dating to the Early Martis, Late Martis, Early Kings Beach, and Late Kings Beach phases.

Material from the Spooner phase and the Early and Late Martis phases was found in Strata 5 and 4. Early Kings Beach phase material was largely found in Strata 3 and 2, and material dating to the Late Kings Beach phase was found in Stratum 2.

The excavation of the Daylight site resulted in a great deal of archaeological data that allow interpretations of what life was like for the people who lived during these six phases. Ethnographic data are also useful in this pursuit. Researchers collect this type of information from living people by observing, listening, and asking questions. Written accounts of this information describe, document, and analyze various cultures and subcultures. Much of what we know about Paiute and Washoe lifeways in the early to mid-twentieth century, some sixty years or more after the first contact with European Americans, comes from such descriptions. These texts are based on the testimony of informants who are no longer living and who were conveying information about the past handed down to them from their parents and grandparents, or from more distant ancestors via oral history. Archaeologist Steven Simms argued that a modern baseline that begins at the point of first contact between indigenous Americans and Europeans must be employed in order to interpret the lives of those who came before.[6] The baseline for this project is situated in the Truckee Meadows and the Eastern Sierra Front. Archaeologists use ethnographic data to establish a baseline, but they cannot assume that precontact peoples lived in a pristine state that had not changed for thousands of years. Nor can the conditions present during the contact period be projected directly back in time as a way of understanding the ancient past. Nevertheless, such ethnographic texts are useful in tandem with archaeological data.

Approximately 5,300 years ago someone dug a shallow pit in the sand near a bend in the river and built a fire with cottonwood branches. Natural processes such as flooding probably filled the pit rapidly with sediment, which preserved its contents for more than five millennia. We do not know who camped here, where they came from, or where they went. We know only that someone built a fire, probably cooked and ate a meal, disposed of the bones of a rabbit in the hearth, and sharpened or reduced a stone tool made of chert.

The archaeological evidence from this hearth feature suggests just how different the world of the campers by the river 5,300 years ago was from the one the region's modern residents know. The differences are not simply because these early residents hunted and gathered on foot rather than driving to the grocery store for sustenance, or because they used chipped stone instead of a steel knife to prepare the food. The differences are fundamental and include a different worldview.

## SPOONER PHASE

The evidence for the occupation of the Daylight site during the Spooner phase, which began approximately 8,000 years ago and ended approximately 5,000 years ago, is limited to the single fire pit or hearth in Stratum 5 described above. The hearth was a shallow pit in the sand about two feet in diameter that was filled with burned rock, charcoal, bones, and artifacts. Charcoal recovered from the hearth produced a calibrated

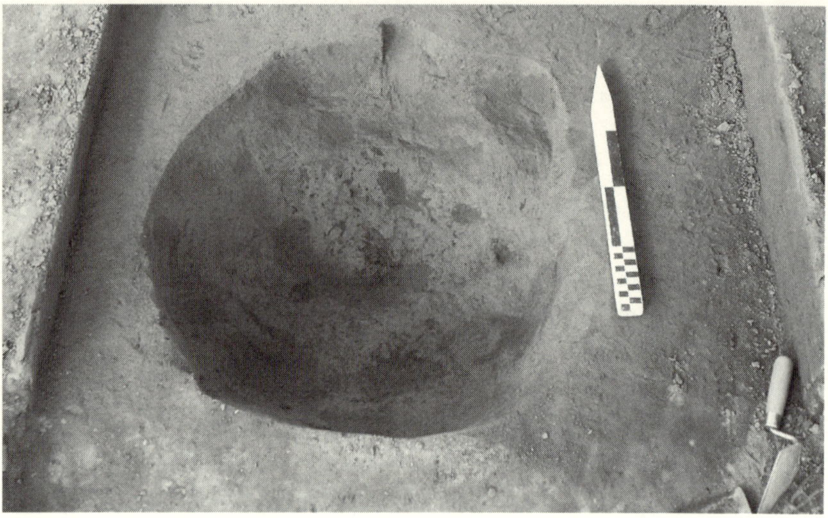

Spooner phase hearth after excavation. Courtesy of WCRM, Inc.

radiocarbon age of 5,310–4,980 BP. In addition to the charcoal and rock, the feature contained seven small chert flakes and five bones from a rabbit.

The Middle Holocene occupation represented by this rare Spooner phase feature is noteworthy. In fact, as of this writing it is the only radiocarbon-dated human-made feature of this age ever found in the Truckee Meadows. An important Early Holocene deposit is a thick layer of volcanic ash that washed from the slopes of Peavine Mountain and was deposited at the confluence of Keystone Canyon and the Truckee River in what is now downtown Reno. It was noted during trench construction elsewhere on the project, near West Street. The ash layer lies about twelve feet below the present ground surface and dates to the eruption of Mount Mazama approximately 7,600 years ago. This has important implications for future research; it demonstrates that both Early and Middle Holocene deposits are preserved along the river and suggests that there may be archaeological sites deeply buried within these deposits.

The transition from Middle to Late Holocene marks a period of dramatic change; moisture increased, seasons became more distinct, reduced annual evaporation resulted in lakes returning to many western basins, and Lake Tahoe reached its natural sill and overflowed into the Truckee River.[7] It was during this time that the river regularly overtopped its shallow Middle Holocene channel and continued to deposit the silts and sands that form the sedimentary sequence at the Daylight site.

### EARLY AND LATE MARTIS PHASES

The Early Martis phase in the Truckee Meadows lasted from 5,000 to 3,000 BP and was a period of increasing population growth and cultural complexity; this pattern has been noted for the Eastern Sierra Front as well as other parts of the Great Basin.[8] The Early Martis phase on the Daylight site is found in Stratum 4 and is represented by two dated features: a hearth with a calibrated radiocarbon age of 4,850–4,800 BP and a bell-shaped storage cist, or pit, under the floor of a house, with a calibrated radiocarbon age of 3,320–3,050 BP.

Martis phase houses were semisubterranean and consisted of a pit with steep side walls dug two to three feet below the ground. Upright posts set in deep holes in the floor supported a roof of willow branches covered with bundled bulrushes. The houses had internal hearths, indicating that they were used in cold weather. Martis phase house floors also included storage pits in which occupants cached food and equipment.

Martis house pit with hearth (*foreground*) and cache pit (*background*), after excavation. The white board in the photo is used to document feature data. Courtesy of WCRM, Inc.

Steamboat dart points from the Daylight site. Courtesy of WCRM, Inc.

The Early Martis phase house at the Daylight site had a hard-packed clay floor and three internal features: two shallow, charcoal-stained pits that were likely hearths, and one storage pit. The side walls were straight and the storage pit was at least two feet deep. The house appears to have been reoccupied a thousand years or so later during the Late Martis phase: a fourth feature, a shallow charcoal stained pit in the Early Martis house floor, was found to have a calibrated date range of 2,150–1,980 BP, much later than the date from the storage cist.

Artifacts found in the house pit fill included a Steamboat type projec-

Elko series dart points from the Daylight site. Courtesy of WCRM, Inc.

tile point. Several of these points were found in Martis phase sediments on the site. Steamboat and Elko series points once tipped spear shafts and were delivered with an atlatl, or spear thrower. Martis phase hunters procured tool stone to make these dart points and other stone tools from local sources such as the Steamboat Springs area, located approximately 9 miles to the south. From this source they got both pink sinter, a type of chert, and black basalt tool stone. They also procured chert tool stone from the Virginia and Pah Rah ranges 12 miles to the east, and basalt tool stone from sources near Truckee and Gold Lake, California, approximately 32 miles to the northwest. Obsidian came from sources 99–130 miles to the south and 81–165 miles to the north.

Obsidian and basalt derive from volcanic deposits. Because individual volcanic eruptions possess unique characteristics, obsidian and basalt from particular sites return a distinctive chemical signature, or "fingerprint," when they are subjected to geochemical analyses such as X-ray fluorescence (XRF). Over the past thirty years geochemists have amassed a large library of signatures from these sources. Artifacts from archaeological sites can be tested using XRF, and often the source of the tool stone from which the tool or projectile point is made can be determined. At the Daylight site, we identified eight obsidian sources and three basalt sources using XRF.

The presence of hunting tools made of tool stone from sources both near and far, along with bones from large game animals such as deer, antelope, and mountain sheep confirms that hunting was indeed important to the occupants of the Daylight site during Martis phase times. For many years archaeologists interpreted such patterns of tool stone procurement to mean that people occupied large territories and moved their residences frequently in pursuit of highly ranked resources such as large game animals. Scientifically, resources are considered to be valuable or highly ranked if their caloric yield exceeds the caloric cost of obtaining them, which includes search, pursuit, and "handling" costs such as retrieval and processing. Archaeological research done more than two decades ago indicated that hunting in general produces an energy benefit that far outweighs that of plant collecting, and that the hunting of large game outweighs small mammal hunting.[9]

This view of highly mobile groups pursuing large game across vast territories has since been challenged. Some researchers point to evidence for substantial sites containing formal house structures, diverse artifact assemblages, and extensive midden or trash deposits found all across the Great Basin and eastern California dating to the Middle Archaic period (5,000–1,300 BP).[10] These sites are indicative of semisedentary or at least multiseason occupation akin to "villages." This village pattern appears to be the rule rather than the exception. For example, archaeologist Robert Elston identified a number of residential base camps with large accumulations of midden and artifacts on the Mount Rose Fan in southwestern Reno.[11] People reoccupied such sites on a consistent basis throughout the Middle Archaic.

The Daylight site contained a formal house structure that may have been regularly reused over a long period; the house and its contents strongly suggest that it was part of a village. During the post-European American contact period, traditional villages had two to ten houses occupied by single families and extended families that were related genetically and by marriage. The house pit and its associated sediments contained different types of grinding stones, including manos and metates, hammer stones, hand stones, nether stones, and pigment-grinding tools. Manos and metates are used to grind food; the metate is a stationary grinding slab, and the mano is held in the hand and used against the metate. Hammer stones are percussors used to pound or to remove flakes from other stones. Hand stones are like manos, and nether stones are like metates, but they are used to grind materials other than food, such as pigments.

Only one house pit was found on the Daylight site, but only a small part of what is undoubtedly a much larger site was actually uncovered. In the Washoe village pattern that may have been established between 1,300 and 150 years ago, winter houses, or *galis dangal,* and winter villages, or *angale atega,* were typically spaced along a stream or clustered close to a spring. The villages contained two to seven houses spaced anywhere from fifty to three hundred feet apart.[12] This spacing allowed for both privacy and security against attack by outsiders. There is little evidence regarding the spacing of Martis phase houses, but it is conceivable that space was maintained between them. In any case, the presence of a house and a diverse chipped and ground stone artifact assemblage in Stratum 4 is evidence of a variety of activities associated with a more stable residential pattern.

The features such as hearths and storage pits within the house pit indicate winter occupation, as do the bones from migratory waterfowl. Waterfowl are abundant in the Truckee Meadows during the fall and early winter, and often use the river as a stopover on their southern migrations. The grinding stones found in Stratum 4 suggest the processing of small, hard-seeded plant species such as dropseed, ricegrass, buckwheat, saltbush, and tansy mustard that would have been harvested in late spring and early summer. Small numbers of fish bones and freshwater mussel shell fragments were also present in the house pit sediments. Fish might have been taken year-round, and mussels would have been harvested during the late summer and early fall, when water levels in the river were low. This is strongly indicative of a multiseason occupation of Daylight during the Early and Late Martis phases. The village-like nature of the site's Martis phase features invites a discussion about the probable division of labor and gender roles at the site.

In keeping with traditional Western gender roles, nineteenth-century anthropologists such as Emile Durkheim maintained that certain aspects of the division of labor were universal and determined by human nature. Tasks were coordinated and distributed by age and gender. Women cooked; took care of the children, the sick, and the elderly; and minded the internal comfort of the home. Men made a living and provided security. Anthropologists who studied living hunter-gatherers using a feminist theoretical framework in the late 1960s and early 1970s, however, found that the focus of early ethnographies on "Man the Hunter" did not square with nutritional analyses. It turned out that while the assumptions about gender roles were largely accurate—men usually hunted and women usually gathered—much higher proportions of the diet were provided by "Woman the Gatherer" than by "Man the Hunter."

Archaeologists have traditionally placed a great deal of emphasis on hunting and hunting implements, again in keeping with traditional Western gender roles. This perspective was further skewed by differential preservation of materials in the archaeological record: stone survives, whereas wood and fiber usually do not. Such traditionally "male" artifacts as projectile points are thus much more common at archaeological sites than traditionally "female" artifacts such as digging sticks and baskets. Modern archaeological work is still hampered by this differential preservation, but archaeologists no longer assign stone tools more importance simply because such tools are more common than wooden ones.

Some studies of prehistoric human remains do suggest a gendered division of labor that seemed to be rooted primarily in reproduction. According to this view, women were more likely to be restricted in their long-distance movements simply because they were busy bearing, breastfeeding, and caring for young children; men were more mobile and traveled longer distances. This view is supported by a study of human skeletal remains from sites in the Carson Sink, about sixty miles east of Reno, that determined that the men had a much higher incidence of joint wear than the women did.[13] More convincing evidence comes from ethnographic studies of modern and historical hunter-gatherer groups that found men more likely to hunt and women more likely to gather. For these reasons, archaeologists usually assert that prehistoric hunter-gatherers established residential bases in areas that facilitated food gathering by women, who were providing the greatest proportion of food for the group as a whole.

The evidence associated with both multiseason occupation of villages and long-distance hunting thus argues for a division of labor along gender lines at the Daylight site. Women and elders stayed close to home, raising the children and providing the staple foods for the group's subsistence, which they obtained by foraging in numerous ecological zones for diverse and abundant local food supplies such as hard seeds and roots. Although providing meat from highly ranked resources such as big game may have brought some prestige to men, such activities usually did not provide the majority of the food needed for the group. Men engaged in long-distance trips away from the village to hunt large game, procure and trade for tool stone, and search for mates. Marrying outside the group not only kept the gene pool healthy and viable, it also helped to establish and strengthen ties with distant groups. These relationships might be useful in times of local resource shortages, when families would have the option to visit their relatives in areas with more abundant resources. In summary, men and women had contrasting but complementary foraging goals, and they chose to live in places like the Daylight site, in a rich and diverse environment that facilitated both women's foraging activities and men's distant forays.

People occupied the Daylight site sporadically between 2,000 and 1,260 BP (during the Late Martis phase) and intensively between 1,260 and 1,160 BP (during the Early Kings Beach phase), when the climate in the Great Basin generally became warmer and drier.[14] Greasewood gave way to pine, sagebrush, grass, and marsh species.[15] Pine increased in abundance relative to juniper between 1,400 and 900 BP, and pinyon pine became an important component of the semiarid woodland and a vital food source in the northwestern Great Basin.

### EARLY KINGS BEACH PHASE

The Early Kings Beach phase, which lasted from 1,300 to 700 BP along the Eastern Sierra Front, falls within the Late Archaic period. It heralded a number of cultural changes, including the introduction of the bow and arrow, a preference for chert tool stone over other types, and smaller tools. People built smaller houses in shallow, dish-shaped depressions and began using stone hullers and bedrock mortars to process pine nuts. Small game and fish became more important in the diet. Although people continued to occupy ecological "sweet spots" such as the Daylight site, they also lived in less optimal locations. This use of formerly unoccupied locations suggests that the population was growing and people were using a wider variety of resources in terms of both subsistence and the places they chose to live. Pinyon pine expanded to its northwestern limit in the Virginia Range between 1,200 and 710 years ago, and many of the sites in formerly unoccupied areas are related to the seasonal gathering of pinyon seeds, commonly known as pine nuts.

Nineteen features were associated with the Early Kings Beach phase at the Daylight site. Of these, eight were radiocarbon dated between 1,280 and 970 BP. Early Kings Beach artifacts and features were initially deposited on—and were intrusive to—Stratum 4, though they were spread throughout Stratum 3 and extended above its upper contact. The disper-

Early Kings Beach rock-lined hearth, excavation in progress. The white board in the photo is used to document feature data. Courtesy of WCRM, Inc.

sion of the Early Kings Beach material was caused by two factors: relatively brief though intensive site use, and the rapid sedimentary deposition of Stratum 3. Possibly as few as two flood events were enough to disperse the material. Thirteen of the nineteen features were hearths, and of these, four were rock filled and two were rock lined. None of the features identified were house pits. Early Kings Beach phase features also included three rock clusters, two large pits, and a possible sunshade/windbreak.

The presence of rock-lined hearths suggests that women processed roots and tubers on the Daylight site. Nutritious plants such as camas (*Camassia quamash*) were probably available on the valley floor. Foods of this type required processing to make them edible and to preserve them for future use. Postcontact ethnographic studies indicate that a bulb like camas would probably have been treated as follows. Preparation began when the women harvested and transported the bulbs to a processing site, probably at the main camp. Pits three to five feet in diameter and about one and one-half feet deep were dug in the soft sand, and dry cottonwood and pine driftwood placed in each pit. The women placed stones atop the dry wood and started fires to heat them. When the fires had burned down and the stones glowed almost red, the stones were moved to form a level surface and covered with a layer of grass. The bulbs, stripped of their outer coats, were laid in a conical pile atop the hot stones, covered with another layer of grass about two or three inches thick, and sprinkled with water. The water generated great clouds of steam, causing some of the rocks below to crack and break. The processors then covered the pile with a layer of earth, built another fire on top of that, and kept it burning until the bulbs were cooked.

The following day the steamed bulbs were removed from the ovens; some would have been eaten as is, but most were pounded using mortars, pestles, manos, and metates until they were reduced to the consistency of dough. This dough was formed into pieces weighing several pounds that were rolled in grass, steamed again, and shaped into cakes of various shapes and sizes from one-half inch to three-fourths inch thick. These were put on drying racks in the sun or smoked over fires. The dried cakes, stored moisture free, could be kept for many months, and along with many other dried and ground seeds harvested from the valley formed the basis for almost every dish the women prepared.

While we do not know if the people who produced the roasting features found at the Daylight site roasted bulbs in the exact way described above, the presence of those roasting features and food-grinding implements within Stratum 3 of the Daylight site suggests that their work was both informed and cooperative. Through trial, failure, and success, humans shaped this place and the world around them just as they do today.

Stratum 3 also contained a possible ramada—an open or semienclosed shelter roofed over with brush or branches. In postcontact times, people built such structures as shields from the sun and wind, a matter of primary importance during the high desert summer and fall. An example is the Washoe *gadu,* or summer shelter. The presence of such a feature might indicate late summer or early fall occupation of the site.

The small and medium-sized rock-filled pits found in Stratum 3 may have originally been hearths, but they were later used as trash pits; in some cases they contained intentionally broken ground stone and ocher-stained ground stone. The large pits may have originally functioned as storage or cache pits but were also ultimately filled with detritus such as fragmentary animal bone, debitage (the small flakes that result when people make or sharpen stone tools), and broken tools, as well as fire-cracked rock, grinding stones for food, and ocher-stained grinding stones. One of the pits also contained human remains.

The presence of intentionally broken ground stone and grinding stones rubbed and coated with red ocher in direct association with human remains is strongly suggestive of ritual behavior. Red ocher is a commonly occurring clay-rich mineral containing hematite, a type of iron oxide. Although people have also used red ocher for a number of practical purposes, cultures worldwide have long used it in ritual contexts, and it is often found in association with human remains. The practice of intentionally breaking tools such as grinding stones as offerings or to

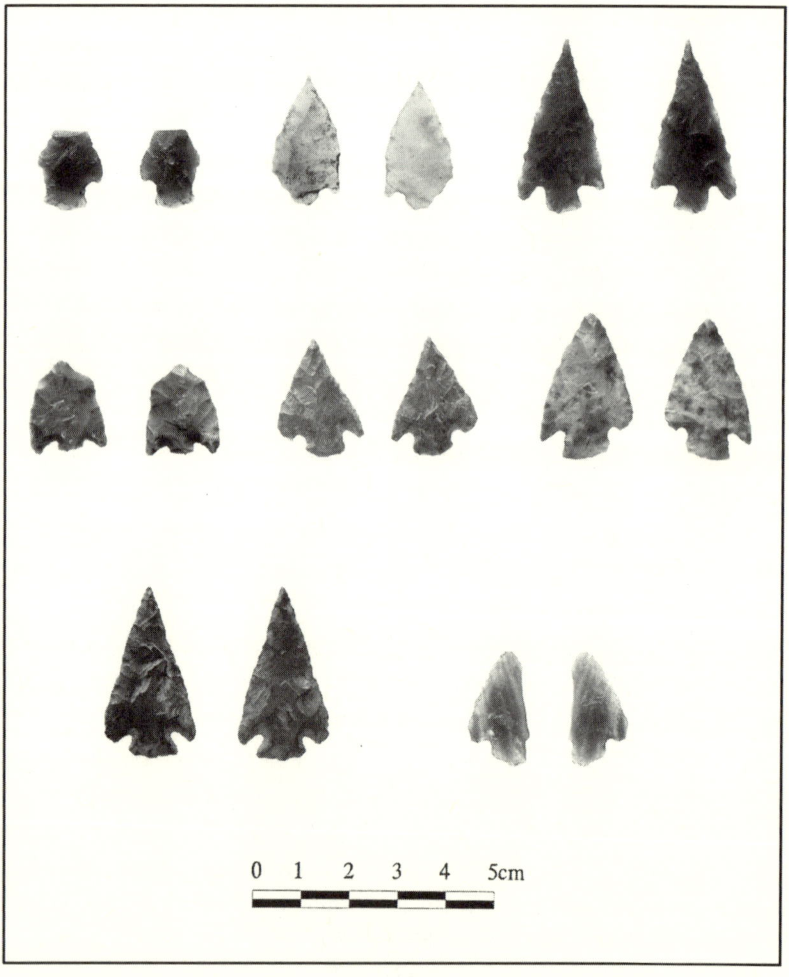


Rosegate series arrow points from the Daylight site. Courtesy of WCRM, Inc.

protect the living from their power after the owner dies is also common in many cultures throughout the world. Scattered human remains were present throughout Strata 3 and 4, and three tightly flexed, cairn-covered pit burials were also part of the Early Kings Beach component. These burials and the significance of intentionally broken and ocher-stained or -coated ground stone are discussed below.

Rosegate projectile points mark the Late Archaic Early Kings Beach phase. Eight of these small, corner-notched arrow tips were found at the site, six made of chert and two of obsidian. The obsidian points came from Sutro Springs, approximately twenty-one miles to the southeast. During the Early Kings Beach phase, people apparently no longer used the more distant obsidian sources they used during the Martis phase. They also rarely used basalt for flaked stone tools. The focus shifted to intensive use of chert and, and to a lesser extent, obsidian, which was available from sources located on the edge of the Truckee Meadows and near Dayton.

The overall subsistence-settlement framework during the Early Kings Beach phase shifted toward intensive collecting and processing of locally available resources, especially roots, seeds, and small game. Evidence for this strategy at the Daylight site included an increase in the number of ground stone implements used to process hard seeds. The Early Kings Beach phase features also contained more than 90 percent of the site's identifiable economically important seeds, including ricegrass, sunflower, tansy mustard, and cattail. The site contained no pine nuts, acorns, or hullers for processing pine nuts.

In addition to the manos and metates used to grind hard seeds and the hand stones and nether stones used for other processing tasks, the Early Kings Beach component contained a significant number of red ocher–stained and red ocher–covered ground stone artifacts. Some of these tools were used to grind red or black pigments. Others appeared to have been marked or painted. None of the red ocher–stained or red ocher–covered ground stone was burned, and more than half of these artifacts were found in features along with intentionally broken, unstained ground stone.

In two cases, intentionally broken ground stone and ocher-coated ground stone were found in direct association with human remains. An intentionally broken metate was in one of the intact graves, and an ocher-stained nether stone lay directly on top of a single human sternum

Intentionally broken ground stone from the Daylight site. Courtesy of WCRM, Inc.

(breastbone) buried in the center of a large refuse pit. These are two of the seventeen locations of human remains found on the Daylight site, thirteen of which were scattered throughout the site sediments and may represent burials that were disturbed by rodents or scavenging animals, dispersed by natural processes such as flooding, or disturbed by people involved in later activities on the site such as digging pits for hearths or roasting ovens. The other four were intact and relatively undisturbed formal burials. Three are associated with the Early Kings Beach phase and were located in Stratum 3. The fourth formal burial likely dates to the Late Kings Beach phase and was found in Stratum 2. This secondary inhumation, or bundle burial, consisted of several human bones buried together.

It is not known if the three individuals buried in formal graves on the Daylight site were genetically related. The three graves were, however, similar; each person was buried in a shallow pit lined with charcoal-stained sediments, and each body was tightly flexed in a fetal position and lay on its right side, with the head facing toward the east. The graves were all in Stratum 3 and were oriented in a line north to south. They were completely covered with large cobbles, and upon their initial exposure appeared to be rock-lined or rock-filled hearths like others on the site. It quickly became obvious that this was not the case. The northernmost grave, Feature 28, contained the remains of a woman in her late twenties. She was buried with an intentionally broken metate, a mano, and a bone awl. The next grave in line to the south held a man likely in his late forties. He was buried with a large rock, approximately the size of a basketball, placed over his head, but without personal possessions. The southernmost grave was that of a child. The sex is unknown, but skeletal analysis indicated that he or she died within the first five years of life. This grave also did not contain any artifacts.

Formal graves like the ones found on the Daylight site are not common in the Truckee Meadows, but graves found in Late Archaic period sites near Steamboat Springs, nine miles to the south, and near Bordertown, eighteen miles to the northwest, are similar in terms of the orientation of the bodies and the burials in pits under piled rocks.[16]

As mentioned above, thirteen other loci of human remains were present in Stratum 3, and eleven of them had been scattered and dispersed by natural and cultural processes. An individual sternum from an adult was found in a large pit, buried beneath a red pigment–stained grinding stone, suggesting that some kind of ritual was performed here. The pit

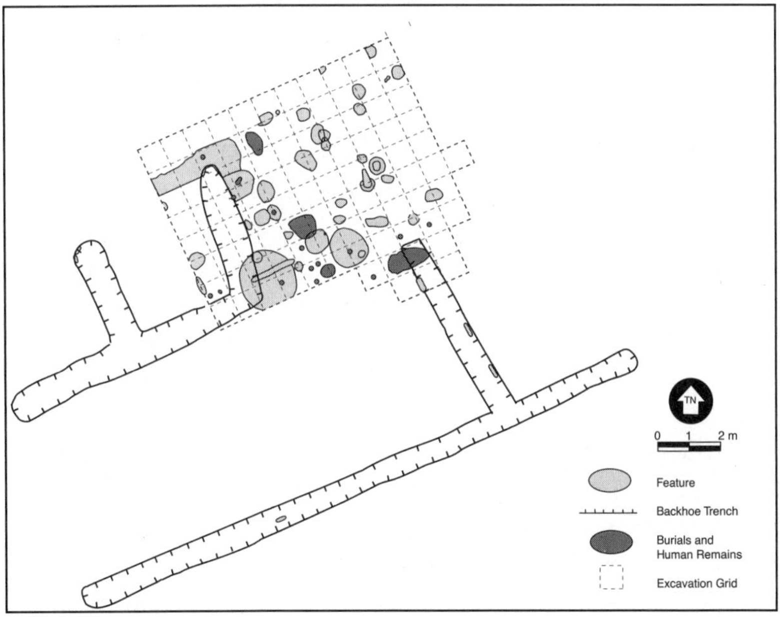


Site overview showing locations of features; the dark features are burials and human remains. Courtesy of WCRM, Inc.

also contained numerous burned and unburned cobbles, broken ground stone, faunal bone, broken stone tools and flakes, and charcoal and burned seeds.

### LATE KINGS BEACH PHASE

The Late Kings Beach phase, dating between 700 and 150 years ago, marks the end of the prehistoric period. The people who occupied the site during this phase were likely the direct ancestors of the Washoe and Northern Paiute groups the first European American explorers and settlers encountered along the Truckee in the 1840s. Late Kings Beach features and artifacts at the Daylight site were generally confined to the surface of Stratum 3 or buried within Stratum 2. Stratum 2 was deposited on a surface that had been stable for several hundred years and was composed of flood deposits that originated from the terraces to the north and not from overbank flooding of the Truckee River. The last millennium in the northern and western Great Basin was characterized by droughts ending at 900, 600, and 350 BP, interspersed with wet intervals.[17] It is likely that the Daylight site was occupied during relatively wet intervals when water was available in the river as it passed through the Truckee Meadows. Late Kings Beach phase occupation of the Daylight site, however, appears to have been much less intensive than in the preceding Early Kings Beach phase.

Eleven features were associated with the Late Kings Beach occupation of the site. Three of these produced calibrated radiocarbon ages bracketed between 560 and 270 BP. Six were rock clusters, three of which contained ground stone; four were hearths, three of which were rock lined or rock filled; and one was a large, deep pit. The purpose of the rock clusters is unknown. The presence of rock-lined or -filled hearths suggests that root and bulb processing continued into the Late Kings Beach phase at the site, and the presence of manos and metates indicates that grinding of hard seeds was still important.

Time-diagnostic artifacts in the Late Kings Beach phase component were limited to one Desert Side notched projectile point and one Cottonwood Triangular projectile point. Ocher-stained ground stone was present, but only two of the twenty-nine pieces recovered from the site were found in association with Late Kings Beach sediments or features. One burial was found: a secondary inhumation consisting of several small skeletal elements including vertebra and collar bone fragments, part of

Railroad bed (dark rocky material) over original ground surface (lighter sandy matrix). The white board in the photo is used to document feature data. Courtesy of WCRM, Inc.

a pelvis, arm bones, and finger and toe bones. The bones were clustered tightly in a small area about twenty centimeters (eight inches) in diameter, and lay atop a bed of small pebbles. They had probably been wrapped or bundled, but no trace of any wrapping material remained. Given the presence of formal burials and human remains in the strata below, it is likely that Late Kings Beach people disturbed some of these remains, perhaps in the course of digging a pit, and reinterred them.

The arrival of European Americans in the Truckee Meadows in the early 1840s changed the lives of the Native American residents forever. The Daylight site may have seen limited occupation after this time, as suggested by a single rock-lined hearth found at the contact point of Strata 1 and 2. Several pieces of chipped stone and a few pieces of ground stone, including a large grinding slab, lay on what would have been the ground surface when Central Pacific built its railroad grade through the area. Fortunately, the construction of the railroad through Reno in 1867–68 had little effect on the site because workers did not dig into the ground. Construction consisted of adding fill material to create the rail bed and little to no modification to the existing surface. This action effectively capped the Daylight site, preserving it essentially undisturbed for the next 136 years. While the landscape of Reno changed dramatically over that time period, the oldest site known to exist in the city lay untouched under the railroad tracks.

BEFORE ANY GROUND WAS BROKEN on the ReTRAC project, the federal government consulted with interested parties, including Native American tribes, regarding their concerns about the project's effects on places important to them. During the initial consultation between the federal government and the tribal governments of the Reno-Sparks Indian Colony, the Washoe Tribe of Nevada and California, and the Pyramid Lake Paiute Tribe, the tribes did not express any concerns. Upon the discovery of the first prehistoric site and, shortly thereafter, the Daylight site, the government notified the tribes, who sent representatives to visit the discoveries. When these representatives expressed concern that the sites might contain human remains, an individual from the Reno-Sparks Indian Colony was assigned to monitor the archaeological excavations. Later, an individual from the Washoe Tribe of Nevada and California also joined the crew as a monitor.

The first human remains discovered at the Daylight site consisted of a long bone found protruding from a rodent burrow more than three feet below the historical railroad bed. Archaeologists immediately contacted a forensic anthropologist, who confirmed that the bone was a human fibula (lower leg bone) and that the remains were ancient, not recent. This initial find later turned out to be associated with the grave of the woman in her twenties found several feet away. The discovery of human remains initiated a complex series of procedures, eventually leading to excavation, repatriation, and reinterment.[18]

Archaeologists collaborated with the tribes, the city of Reno, the Nevada Department of Transportation, and the Federal Highway Administration on a plan to excavate, remove, scientifically study, and reinter the human remains from the site. This plan provided a framework for procedures to follow whenever human remains were discovered during the project and ensured that the remains would be reinterred in the Daylight site after the project was completed. Ultimately, human remains were recovered from three intact or primary graves, one secondary inhumation, and other scattered locations in the site, as discussed above. Taking all these loci into account, it was determined that at least five individuals were buried on the site. Following the plan, researchers cataloged and studied the remains but took no photographs and performed no destructive tests. The forensic anthropologist recorded the remains by taking standard measurements, shading standard forms, and drawing illustrations by hand.

More testing, such as DNA analysis, would have allowed many more questions to be addressed. For example, were the three people buried in the formal graves genetically related? Was the secondary burial found in the Late Kings Beach phase sediments related to the Early Kings Beach burial? Were any of the individuals buried on the site related to the modern Washoe or Paiute, or were they related to another group or groups entirely? DNA analysis might have answered these questions, but in order to test human bone, a small amount would have to be destroyed in the process. The tribes were opposed to this and generally were not interested in addressing questions of ancestry. They believe that the creator placed them here and that they have always been in this place. In the resulting compromise by both parties, some of the project's scientific goals were met, the human ancestors were treated with respect, and multiple interests came together in the process.

On 12 December 2004, representatives of the tribes, the state and federal governments, the city, and WCRM gathered to lay the remains to rest in a ceremony by the river, near where they had been originally buried. Participants offered prayers in Paiute, Washoe, and English and emphasized that they were there to pay respect to those who came before—not as Washoe, Paiute, or Shoshone ancestors, but as human ancestors; respect and reverence for these people transcended cultural affiliation and cultural differences.

Although archaeologists were not able to engage in every possible aspect of scientific research on the project, study of the human remains and the broken and painted ground stone artifacts permitted the investigation of some sacred and ritual aspects of the Daylight site; these included issues such as mortuary practices and the disposal of personal property at death.

The site's Early Kings Beach phase component contained an interesting artifact class: raw lumps of red ocher pigment scattered throughout Stratum 3. As noted, the site's occupants used some of the ground stone artifacts in the Early Kings Beach deposits to grind these pigments. They used others for different purposes, such as grinding food or as hammer

Excavation of an ocher-covered mano. The white board in the photo is used to document feature data. Courtesy of WCRM, Inc.

stones for making stone tools, and they painted or coated some of the artifacts with red ocher. Geochemical testing of the red ocher residue from several of the coated and stained ground stones revealed that the ocher was from volcanic deposits; some samples contained arsenic in concentrations sufficient to cause sickness or even death if consumed. This suggests that the ground stones were coated with such materials as an explicit warning against using or touching them.

The Northern Paiute used red ocher in a number of ways in the post-contact period, including as body paint, in rock art, for coating ceremonial objects such as eagle feathers and rattles, and as protection from the spirits of the dead. The color red had specific importance to some of the tribes involved with the Daylight site, and archaeologists were asked to wrap all of the human remains in red cotton cloth as they were excavated. Tribal representatives also treated the remains with powdered red ocher before reburying them.

Many of the ground stone fragments that were not coated or painted with red ocher showed evidence of having been intentionally broken. More than half of these had been disposed of in old hearths or storage pits, and two, a mano and a metate, were found in the grave of the woman. A red ocher–stained grinding slab was found in direct association with the single human sternum in the old storage pit. The presence of red ocher pigments, ocher-grinding implements, and ocher-stained and -covered ground stone, along with intentionally broken ground stone tools in direct association within human remains, former hearths, and possible storage features, strongly suggests ritual destruction of and disposal of personal property upon death.

The Paiute and many other Native Americans view the earth as a living being; all things in it, including rocks and the minerals used to make paint, contain power, or *puha.* Power is also manifested in things that people make and use. Ethnographer Penny Rucks learned from her work with members of the modern Washoe Tribe that the "Washoe world view restricted access to personal property, including property of the dead, and is related to beliefs about the integration of spirit power," or *wegele'yu.*[19]

The Washoe people used *d'emge?* (a metate or nether stone) in tandem with various *ga'mum* (a mano or hand stone) for grinding or rolling. According to modern Washoe, *d'emge?* and *ga'mum* were personal property, and communal use was rare. *D'emge?* cached on a site in the open was considered "safe" for others to use, but if it was hidden or buried it could not be used. Rucks also learned that broken or scattered *d'emge?,* particularly those missing one or more pieces, were indicators of "mysterious events and a dangerous place."[20] Some personal property of witches, for example, was disposed of in this manner. In the early 1950s, informants who worked with ethnographers Stanley and Ruth Freed indicated that both witches and sorcerers existed among the Washoe.[21] Sorcerers had active control over their *wegele'yu,* whereas a witch was an old person whose generalized power had become strong with age. Sorcerers used their power in conscious acts of malevolence, while witches were "hapless victims of a condition arising naturally from old age."[22] Old people might inadvertently bewitch a child or young person and were sometimes charged with sorcery and killed; their personal property, which also contained power, was also "killed" through breakage. A woman could give her *d'emge?* and *ga'mum* to a relative before dying, but if she died suddenly without distributing her implements, these items became dangerous and had to be ritually cleansed and either broken or thrown into the river.[23]

The distribution of the many ocher-modified artifacts along with the human remains, intentionally broken ground stone, and formal burials at Daylight strongly suggest that ritual activities took place on the site in Early Kings Beach times. Again, the exact meanings of these rituals will never be known, and it is impossible to understand the ancient occupants of this place simply by projecting the beliefs of historically known and modern Native American cultures such as the Washoe and Northern Paiute backward in time. The worldview, spiritual beliefs, and rituals practiced here 1,300 years ago may in fact have been quite different from those practiced by Native Americans of the past two centuries, and were certainly different from those practiced today. During the Early Kings Beach phase, this place by the river was used for mundane tasks such as the processing of roots and the grinding of seeds for subsistence, but it also assumed increasing importance as a place to bury the dead and perhaps to safely dispose of personal possessions that had become too powerful for the living to use.

Daylight site excavation overview. Courtesy of WCRM, Inc.

PRESERVED BENEATH THE RAILROAD TRACKS that run through downtown Reno is an archaeological record spanning more than 5,000 years that encompasses most of the cultural phases defined for the Eastern Sierra Front and represents many generations of sporadic human occupation. People began using this place by the river approximately 5,300 years ago, as evidenced by a single campfire. By Early Martis phase times there were one or more pit houses, and the site may have been the location of multiseasonal occupation or a village that provided a stable base for foraging and hunting. During the Early Kings Beach phase, at least part of the site became a locus of mortuary and ritual practices. In the Late Kings Beach phase occupation, people continued to use the site as a camp and as a place to process roots and seeds, but to a much lesser extent than in the previous period.

The Daylight site is the first deeply stratified site identified and excavated in the Truckee Meadows. It is extremely important because it indicates that early Holocene geomorphic features such as levees are preserved under the present floodplain, which may very well contain deeply buried Early and Middle Holocene archaeological sites as well. Such sites may be virtually untouched by modern development, even those in urban environments. Of the eighty-three archaeological sites found by the ReTRAC project, the Daylight site was by far the oldest; it was and is also the best preserved. The physical traces of the past preserved in the site provide a great deal of information about how people made a living in an ever-changing environment. Remarkably, they also provide insight into a rich spiritual and ritual life rarely visible in archaeological sites and further strengthen the bridge between the present and the past in this place.

CHAPTER

# 3

## Reno and the Railroad

The traditional image of the "Wild West" usually does not include cities. We picture the *Bonanza* version of Virginia City, perhaps, with its ramshackle false-front wooden buildings and tumbleweed-filled streets, but little else in the way of civilization. Some of the West's small boomtowns did indeed fit that stereotype, experiencing life spans but too short to lead to stable "city" status and being populated predominantly by itinerant males. But the western United States of the late nineteenth century also had a number of sophisticated urban centers that had more in common with the bustling cities of the East than the dusty boardwalks of Tombstone. San Francisco, Sacramento, Portland, Seattle, Denver, and Virginia City were all large, thriving cities during this time, and their residents aspired to the same social and economic markers of success as the inhabitants of other urban centers did.

Reno existed on a smaller scale than the western cities mentioned above, but it too had most of the characteristics of a major urban center. Its railroad supply line closely tied it to the state's largest community, Virginia City, with its Comstock riches. Thanks mostly to its location on the transcontinental railroad line, Reno remained economically strong even when Virginia City's fortunes declined. Reno prided itself on having all the amenities and culture of any proper urban center, and its physical landscape reflected an urban orientation from the town's earliest beginnings.

The term "landscape" has multiple meanings and encompasses more than its common usage implies. Landscapes are physical, social, cultural, and even emotional in nature, and perceptions of them vary from person to person. In Reno as in any other place, the landscape both helps define and is defined by the people who live within it. Because people's influence on their surroundings is ongoing and ever-changing, landscapes are also evolving, dynamic things. Recognizing the distinguishing physical features of urban centers and the artifacts associated with them enables an understanding of what it means to live in a city. Although many people think of landscapes as exclusively rural and scenic, cities are really the clearest reflection of humanity's influence on its natural environment. Urban landscapes can be extremely complex, and Reno's is no exception—yet it can be "read." The layout of its streets, the orientation of its buildings, and the way its neighborhoods relate to one another were all shaped by the context in which Reno was created.

Classifying a community as a town rather than a city is a largely unnecessary exercise when examining an urban landscape. The difference between the two rests in the type of local government, but both are urban in orientation. This book uses both "town" and "city" to refer to Reno because both terms have applied at different times. While each settlement is unique, every urban setting has four important defining characteristics: distinctive demographics, such as a dense population; centralized political and administrative features, such as a municipal government or an infrastructure system; economic features; and social heterogeneity.[1] These characteristics are the essential forces shaping urban areas, and they are visible archaeologically through both artifact distribution patterns and landscape. In the archaeological sense, landscape is explored through studies of land use and management, city structures and buildings, and site formation processes—how natural and cultural forces affect sites over time.

The arrival of the transcontinental railroad was the single most important shaping force in the development of Reno's urban landscape. Before the railroad came through, Reno's location-to-be within the Truckee Meadows was fairly unremarkable and was definitely not urban. The area was home to members of the Washoe and Paiute tribes, ranchers, homesteaders, and entrepreneurs who operated small river crossings and supply stations for emigrants headed to California. The arrival of the railroad in 1868 changed everything. The importance of the railroad to Reno's development may not be obvious today, in a world where the landscape has been altered to accommodate the car. But a reading of Reno's landscape reveals the influence that the nineteenth-century rail industry had

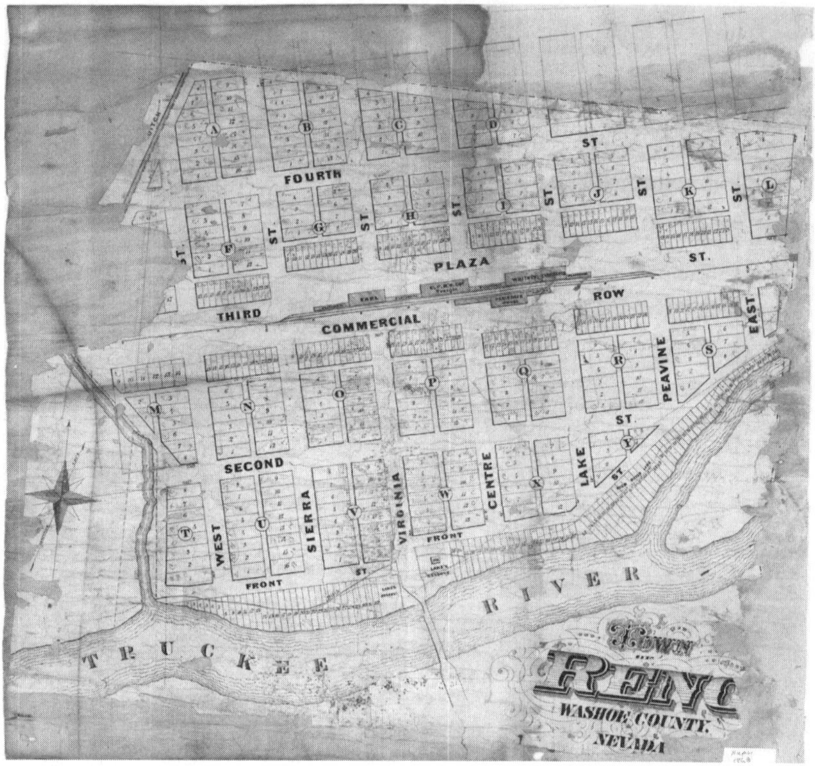


Original Reno townsite, 1868. Courtesy of the Nevada Historical Society and the Mary B. Ansari Map Library.

on the city's appearance and identity—an influence that continues to be felt.

Reno's present-day landscape can be traced back to a stroke of meteorological luck. In 1868 a better-established community, Glendale, sat farther east on the Truckee River and was the logical location for the Central Pacific's new railroad station. But when the railroad surveyors arrived in the Truckee Meadows to pick a site, Glendale happened to be completely flooded thanks to a particularly wet spring and heavy snowmelt. The surveyors decided that a higher location would be more desirable and chose an area farther upriver, at the location of Lake's Crossing.

Workers constructed the transcontinental railroad in two directions: east from Sacramento, California, and west from Council Bluffs, Iowa, with the two lines eventually meeting at Promontory Point, Utah. The eastward construction of the transcontinental line reached Lake's Crossing on 5 May 1868. Central Pacific auctioned off the platted lots of the new townsite of Reno on 9 May. While the main railroad facilities were established farther east at Wadsworth, Central Pacific planned for the Reno station to be the hub for passenger and freight traffic to the booming Comstock. More than one hundred businesses opened between the auction in May and the arrival of the first train one month later.

The *Gold Hill News* described the burgeoning town in July 1868:

> Outside of Gold Hill and Virginia City it is the most stirring town in this state. The railroad has done wonders for the neighborhood—for what was nothing but a barren open plain just three months ago, is now a real, wide-awake, flourishing little town of at least 2,000 inhabitants, with stores, saloons, restaurants, workshops, hay-yards, and immense warehouses, filled with goods and merchandise, and long trains of cars passing and repassing through the place almost hourly. Bully for Reno.[2]

Central Pacific platted the streets of the fledgling city with an eye toward maximizing convenience, control, and profits. Railroad companies at that time were extremely powerful, and many communities lived or died based on where the companies decided to place their sidings and stations. The railroads stood to make large profits from freight and passenger business, so the more control they had over the towns with which they were associated, the better. One historically documented method of minimizing local interference, in Reno and elsewhere, was by limiting the number of railroad crossings in a town.[3] More crossings meant greater potential for accidents, loss of life, loss of profits, and bad public relations for the railroad.

Although Reno was not a company town in the true sense of the term, it was almost completely dependent on the railroad during its early years. Unlike many Nevada towns established during the late nineteenth century, Reno's position as a hub of transcontinental commerce and transportation ensured its survival. The Reno station provided valuable services to passengers traveling to the east and west, and was the main connection between San Francisco and the booming Comstock in Virginia City.

In 1997 cultural geographer Paul F. Starrs, oral historian Jeanne Harrah, and anthropology graduate student Heather Van Wormer produced a study for Union Pacific that examined Reno's historical layout in relation to the railroad's influence. They concluded that Reno's development was unique among western railroad towns because it remained

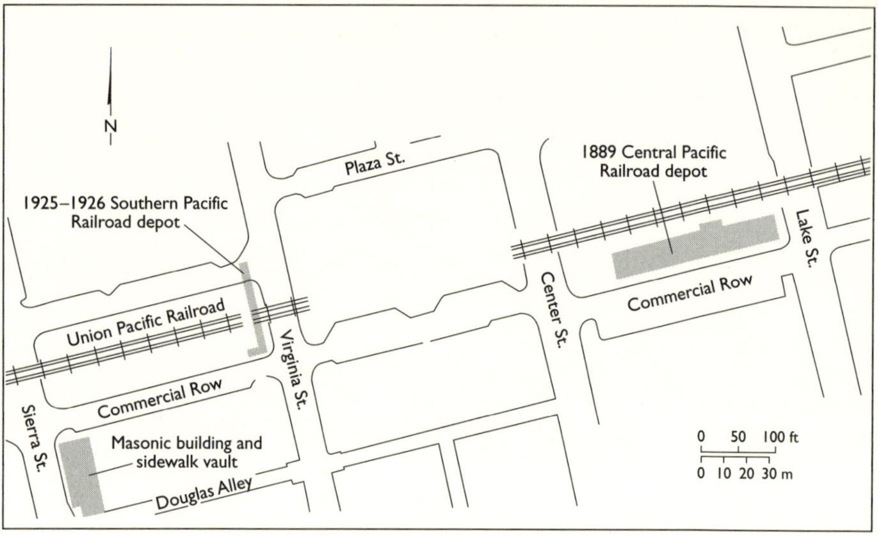


Downtown streets and locations of sites discussed in this chapter.

centered on the railroad tracks. The commercial district eventually expanded north across the tracks, hastened by the establishment of large casinos there in the 1970s and 1980s, resulting in a downtown essentially divided in two by active tracks. In other towns, either the central business district slowly migrated away from the active tracks or the city dealt with the problem by depressing or elevating the tracks much earlier than Reno did.[4]

While Reno would differ from other towns in the middle and late twentieth century, its original nineteenth-century incarnation was a classic demonstration of American railroad development. Nineteenth-century railroad companies not only obtained rights-of-way on which to build their railroad, they also deliberately created townsites and stations along the route to create new patterns of trade and commerce.[5] Reno's modern landscape is thus a direct result of the railroad's planning.

Central Pacific's townsite planning department was responsible for laying out Reno's original street grid, and did so in direct relationship to the railroad's orientation: streets and blocks are not oriented true north–south and east–west, but at angles more northwest–southeast and southwest–northeast, in a perpendicular alignment to the main line tracks. This layout is reflected in the locations and orientations of Reno's infrastructure features, such as fire cisterns and the Virginia Street pedestrian underpass, as well as the modern streets that still follow original routes.

These infrastructure features are addressed in greater detail in this chapter and the next.

Reno's symmetrical plat, with the railroad occupying the center of town, is one of the five or six standard town plans used by the railroads.[6] Since the railroad platted the town to maximize its own profits and convenience, the layout was focused on the daily arrival and departure of trains. It follows that Reno's downtown core was largely designed to reap profits from travelers who were in town for only a short time. Reno's later twentieth-century development as divorce haven and gambling destination was a direct result of this early emphasis on providing services to nonresidents. Residents, of course, used many of the same services and patronized many of the same establishments, because downtown also served as the business core for the local community. This emphasis on trade with train passengers and railroad freight shipping enabled Reno to grow and prosper as a community when other Nevada towns were failing.

Historical photographs show that as many as six parallel sets of tracks ran through downtown Reno during the late nineteenth and early twentieth centuries, occupying a wide swath of land. More tracks were pres-

Main line railroad corridor through downtown Reno, ca. 1899, facing east toward Sierra Street. Courtesy of the Nevada Historical Society.

ent farther east in the rail yards and industrial parcels between Evans Avenue and East (now Record) Street. One historical source reports that fifteen sets of tracks occupied the area by 1897.[7] Additional spurs used by local businesses such as bottlers, meatpacking plants, and lumber yards outside the downtown core diverged from the main line tracks at various points. Many of Reno's commercial and industrial operations, dependent on the spurs and main line for distribution of their goods, provided the railroad with yet another source of income by leasing land within the railroad right-of-way.

Several business blocks set back from the tracks on both sides accommodated freight warehouses and railroad structures. Together with the actual tracks, this setback area created a rail yard approximately 800 feet wide that was reserved solely for railroad-related activities. It contained warehouses, unused rail cars, hardware, open storage lots, even corrals full of cattle on their way to and from markets. The rail yard sat at the center of an urban downtown bustling with businesses, restaurants, bars, wagon (and later car) traffic, and pedestrians. Commercial Row, Reno's most heavily used street and the heart of downtown, was platted back 279 feet in the block south of the passenger depot, creating a right-angle jog around the rail yard.[8] Commercial Row is no longer the main thoroughfare, but its alignment, including the jog south of the passenger depot, is still present in Reno's modern streets.

During the ReTRAC project, archaeologists recorded evidence of at least two passenger depots, railroad signals and crossing gates, and downtown commercial buildings. These sites fell into three property types illustrating the railroad's impact on Reno's urban landscape: (1) railroad buildings, including passenger depots and connected hotels; (2) railroad grade crossings, switches, and signals in relationship to city streets; and (3) commercial buildings dependent on locations close to railroad spur lines. These property types are present in any city that is or was related with a railroad, and they are important in the reading of the urban landscape.

The National Park Service defines a property type as "a grouping of properties defined by common physical and associative attributes."[9] "Property" is used generally to mean a physical entity and can range in scale. A property type contains multiple properties with similar physical characteristics or functions. For example, mine complexes, shafts, tramway systems, trails, and dredges are all types of mining property.

When historical sites, buildings, structures, objects, and districts are categorized within a relevant property type, they can be linked to a historical context, and their significance and integrity can be evaluated. In this way actual physical sites can be tied to abstract, theoretical research questions. Property types are commonly used in the evaluation of sites' eligibility for inclusion in the National Register of Historic Places.

### RAILROAD BUILDINGS

Passenger depots generally exhibit a characteristic, easily recognizable style because the railroad companies repeatedly used the same few standard design plans.[10] Most depots are simple, functional buildings; many incorporate some local flourish such as a native material or a regional style into the standard plan. Some urban depots, especially during the height of rail travel, reached heights of design and construction that can only be described as monumental. New York's Union Station and St. Louis's Union Station are not only beloved landmarks of urban centers, they are also enduring symbols of turn-of-the-century culture, when passenger depots were the most visible, and vital, component of the rail system that changed the face of the country.

The original Central Pacific depot (*center background*) and a freight warehouse (*left foreground*), 1868. The Native American men sit on the warehouse platform. Courtesy of the Nevada Historical Society.

Reno's passenger depot has existed in at least five incarnations, built and rebuilt at the same desirable spot at the center of the original platted town. The ReTRAC project exposed portions of two of these depot incarnations. The history of these buildings shows both the importance of the railroad to Reno and the tenacity of an urban community devastated by fire on multiple occasions.

Reno's first passenger depot was a utilitarian wood frame building constructed in May 1868. Typical of early depots, it was built by the same construction crews that built the tracks themselves and was never meant to be permanent.[11] This depot stood for only a few months before it was replaced by the much grander Depot Hotel, run by William R. Chamberlain.

True to its name, the Depot Hotel contained lodging facilities as well as a passenger depot; it also featured a restaurant and a bar. Its oyster saloon advertised "Oysters in Every Style, Clams, Crabs, Pigs' Feet, Cold Meats, Hot Coffee and Tea, and Other Delicacies."[12] The presence of oyster shell fragments in several of the downtown sites hints at the popularity of this shellfish. Oyster shells may seem odd things to find in a high desert environment, but they are among the most common artifacts found in archaeological sites dating to the nineteenth century. The

The second Depot Hotel, 1886. Courtesy of the Nevada Historical Society.

ubiquity of oyster shell fragments in western boomtowns such as Virginia City led to local perceptions of the shellfish as part of the luxurious, decadent lifestyle of a successful mining town.[13] The lifestyle of the average miner was decidedly unglamorous, however, and while he may have enjoyed the occasional oyster meal, boomtown life was not the lavish champagne-fueled free-for-all popular folklore suggests. If anything, the ubiquity of oyster shells in nineteenth-century sites is a testament to the shell's durability.

The Depot Hotel was an example of a successful partnership between the railroad and a local businessman, as the business was apparently a joint venture. While many railroad depots contained restaurants or cafés operated by a contracted proprietor, for the most part they were owned and controlled exclusively by the railroad. The exact terms of the Depot Hotel's funding and ownership are unknown, but the agreement between Chamberlain and the railroad was probably in the form of a subcontract, wherein the railroad subsidized the construction of the hotel, Chamberlain ran the business, and the two parties divided the profits. Newspaper accounts of the time name Chamberlain as the proprietor of the Depot Hotel, and the business is referred to as "his hotel."[14] The then-unincorporated community of Reno seems not to have played a role in the construction, maintenance, and operation of the Depot Hotel, as newspaper sources do not mention any city connection other than the imposing structure being a point of civic pride.

The Depot Hotel increased in size with several additions and renovations; Chamberlain added a second story in June 1876 and a third story and observation tower just one month later.[15] The building survived the fire of 1873 only to endure another fire in its third story and attic in 1877. Lena Johnson, a twenty-seven-year-old chambermaid at the hotel, died of smoke inhalation in the fire. The conflagration completely destroyed the top floor, on which Mrs. Johnson and two other hotel employees—hostler John Hayes and porter Charles Jackson—lived.[16] Chamberlain quickly had his hotel repaired; the third floor was rebuilt in the same year. The March 1879 fire that leveled most of downtown completely destroyed the Depot Hotel, but the structure was rebuilt again in the same year.

The grand three-story structure built in 1879 had three tower-like cupolas and was a great source of pride for the town. In addition to being the station for both the Central Pacific and Virginia & Truckee railroads, the Depot Hotel contained the offices of Wells Fargo Express Company

Depot Hotel fountain, 1882. Courtesy of the Nevada Historical Society.

and Western Union, a restaurant, a bar, and lodging.[17] An 1879 map indicates that the building also contained a large kitchen, baggage room, waiting room, and hotel office; a separate wood frame building to the east housed a laundry room, storehouse, and poultry house.[18] A wooden platform extended around the hotel, covering much of the open land in the parcel and partially surrounding a park to the west of the building. Newspaper articles from the time mention the park as a good advertisement for Reno and note a particularly beloved fountain.

Backhoe trenching under the Center Street sidewalk exposed the remains of this fountain, a short segment of a cement-covered, curved brick foundation wall that had been broken by previous modern utility work. In January 1882 the *Nevada State Journal* described the ice-covered fountain as "Worth While Seeing": "It would have paid any one for the trouble if they had walked down and looked at the Depot Hotel Fountain yesterday morning. It has been a pleasing sight several times during the winter, but yesterday it was perfectly beautiful."[19]

The Depot Hotel burned down for the final time in May 1889 and was a total loss. Its proprietor at that time, Robert Parry, started meeting with Central Pacific Railroad officials immediately after the fire to negotiate terms for rebuilding. After more than a month of consideration, railroad officials informed Parry that they would not subsidize another depot-hotel combination. By this point Reno had a number of privately owned, high-quality hotels to compete with a railroad-subsidized establishment; as the *Nevada State Journal* put it, "the era of the great railroad public houses has very nearly ended."[20] Central Pacific opted instead to construct a depot facility without a hotel.

The new depot, completed in December 1889, was a one-story, slate-roofed, brick building containing a waiting room, baggage room, Wells Fargo office, and Wells Fargo freight house.[21] The ticket office occupied a rounded portion of the structure protruding from the north wall and had a conical roof. The depot, along with the rest of the railroad facilities, switched to Southern Pacific ownership in 1899.

Sometime between 1899 and 1904, Southern Pacific renovated the depot to include more rooms: a small bedroom and bathroom on the west side, probably for use by employees of Wells Fargo, which still had an office and storeroom in the west side of the building; an enlarged ticket office with room for a telegraph office; a small office and bathroom on the east side, probably for use by Southern Pacific employees and passengers; and separate waiting rooms for men and women—a not uncommon

The 1889 Central Pacific Depot (*left*) and Wells Fargo Express Co. building (*right*), ca. 1906. Courtesy of the Nevada Historical Society.

The 1925–26 Southern Pacific passenger depot. Photo by Mary Ringhoff.

feature of Victorian public buildings.[22] Women traveling without a male escort were usually expected to stay somewhat sequestered during stops; polite society frowned on women entering saloons, even for a drink of water, and dining alone was only slightly more acceptable. There was a definite need for socially acceptable, female-only spaces where travelers could spend time without worrying about bending social rules or exposing themselves to unwanted attention from males. While earlier incarnations of the depot may also have contained gender-segregated spaces, they are not labeled as such on historical maps; the 1899–1904 addition is the first confirmed instance of separate waiting rooms.

By 1906 Wells Fargo had moved into a new brick building west of the main depot and the depot was occupied entirely by Southern Pacific facilities. Additional interior renovations of the main depot continued over the years. In 1913 the ticket office moved to the southern side of the building and gained a second ticket window.[23]

The citizenry did not particularly admire the brick depot's squat, utilitarian appearance, and locals began publicly expressing desire for a new building as early as 1910.[24] After years of rumors, in 1925 Southern Pacific announced construction of a new depot. Demolition of the old depot commenced in early summer 1925. In June a *Sparks Tribune* article reported that "a large gang of men have been steadily employed pulling down the old building for the past three weeks and their work is almost done."[25] Hand-demolishing the building in this way meant that the bricks could be reused in the new depot building. Workers completed the new depot early in 1926, and it became a beloved landmark; many 1920s–30s postcards and images of Reno feature it prominently. It still stands today as an example of the Mediterranean Revival architectural style, with stucco-finished brick walls and red tile roofing. The central terminal area has a gabled roof, and the areas on either side are flat roofed. The well-preserved interior appears much as it would have in 1926, with exposed wooden ceiling beams and the original wooden benches.

Ground-disturbing activities near the depot in 2004 exposed the physical remains of the 1879 Depot Hotel and Wells Fargo office, and of the 1889 depot. They also exposed several subsurface features related to the 1926 depot. Four wall remnants and a distinct burn layer were revealed in the western portion of the depot parcel under an area that once contained the baggage room of the 1926 Southern Pacific Railroad passenger depot. The baggage room had occupied the western end of the building and featured ramped entrances for wheeling luggage carts to and from the platform. Southern Pacific demolished this portion of the building and replaced it with a small attached building in 1966 that housed the Turf Club, a sports-betting establishment. Extensive disturbance related to utility placements, the razing of the baggage room, and the construction of the modern building left only a few buried remnants of the older depot buildings.

The burn layer, representing at least one of the fires known to have swept this part of downtown, contained carbon-stained soil and numerous oyster shell fragments and dated to sometime between 1868 and 1889. It held only a few fragmentary artifacts and could not be tied to a specific incarnation of the Depot Hotel, or to a specific conflagration. The disturbance exposed four wall and foundation fragments: one was brick, two were concrete, and one was mortared cobbles. The features were related to at least two of the lot's earlier occupants: the 1879 Depot Hotel and the small brick building that held the Wells Fargo Express Company operation for a few years after 1906.

The brick foundation wall fragment was a remnant of the short-lived Wells Fargo office. According to the 1906 Sanborn fire insurance map, the Wells Fargo office was a two-story brick building that was irregular in shape, measured about sixty feet long and thirty feet wide, and stood west of the depot. The second story had an iron-clad floor. Iron-clad buildings or rooms were somewhat fire-resistant as well as theft-

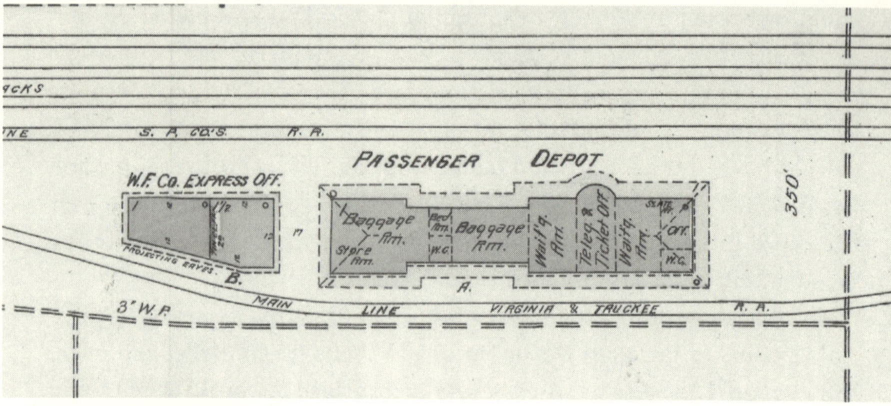

*Top:* The 1889 passenger depot and Wells Fargo Express Company building as shown on the 1906 Sanborn fire insurance map of Reno. Courtesy of the Nevada Historical Society and the Mary B. Ansari Map Library.

*Bottom:* North side of the 1889 depot showing the circular portion of the ticket office. Courtesy of the Nevada Historical Society.

resistant, and this room may have housed the company's more valuable materials. Cast iron façades were also a popular architectural style at the time, although it was somewhat unusual to have such a façade on a building's second story but not the first. The Wells Fargo office did not appear on Sanborn maps after 1918, when the U.S. Railroad Administration consolidated all express companies, including Wells Fargo, into the American Railway Express Company to facilitate the World War I effort. It is unknown whether this action directly affected the Reno Wells Fargo office at that time, but by 1933 only the banking branch of Wells Fargo still existed, and Reno's express business was likely being conducted from the American Railway Express office (1925) about a block away.

The mortared cobble wall segment found in the parcel's western portion was a foundation wall of the 1879 Depot Hotel. Unfortunately, its fragmentary nature and the lack of associated artifacts and features meant that it did not offer much useful information aside from what was already known from archival research.

In the eastern part of the parcel, directly underneath and next to the standing depot, ground disturbances exposed seven additional depot-related features. Two of them were brick vestiges of the 1889 Central Pacific depot. One short segment of brick foundation wall was exposed directly beneath the floor of the current depot during removal of part of the concrete slab floor, but it was too small to be interpreted as anything more than a remnant of the 1889 depot. The other vestige was a circular brick wall extending outward from the standing depot's northern wall. Examination of historical photographs showed that it was the distinctive circular exterior wall of the 1889 depot's ticket office. Demolition of the 1889 depot and the subsequent construction of the 1926 depot had damaged the ticket office wall, basically cutting it off at each end, but it was still recognizable. The archaeological remnants of the 1889 depot confirm that the building's foundations were not completely removed before the new depot was constructed on top of them.

The 1926 depot and the associated American Railway Express and Southern Pacific freight house buildings were nominated for listing in the National Register in 1983, but listing did not occur because the owner, Southern Pacific Railroad, objected.[26] The proposed excavation of the ReTRAC trench put all three of these railroad buildings in jeopardy. Recognizing the inherent value of these historical buildings, the city of Reno decided to preserve them in place by shoring up their foundations and stabilizing them on the edge of the new railroad trench. Architects designed a new addition to the western end of the depot, where the baggage room originally was, to allow rail passengers to board trains at the bottom of the trench. The new portion was designed in the same Mediterranean style as the original building to match the historical character of the 1926 depot. Today, the walls of this lower addition display photographs of the previous depot incarnations.

Reno's plans for the Southern Pacific depot perfectly illustrate the idea of "adaptive reuse" of existing buildings for modern purposes. Today the

Underpinning of the depot during trench construction. Courtesy of WCRM, Inc

depot is intact, in good condition, and vibrant with use. Most important, it still reflects the experience of rail travel that has shaped the town for 140 years. Like other historical buildings, the depot is more than just a static, unchanging object; it is a crucial component of the urban landscape. Historical preservationist Norman Tyler suggested looking at the preservation of old buildings in terms of nouns and verbs:

> When buildings are viewed as objects, they are nouns. . . . Thinking of historic landmarks in terms of their physical structure is the most prevalent viewpoint. But they should be seen as more than that. If they also are seen as places of involvement—where historic events took place—then we can see them also as verbs.
>
> Just as nouns and verbs are both needed to make a complete sentence, both the noun and verb aspects of historic buildings are needed to describe their full significance. Preservationists need to recognize that the preservation of historic buildings should include not only the physical structure but also the history of the place. Only in this way does a historic building maintain its full meaning. To consider the spaces within and around buildings as part of their living history allows historic structures a more active and significant role within the community.[27]

There are tangible benefits to historic preservation as well—economic as well as social and cultural. Cities that have preserved and revitalized portions of their historic downtowns have created successful new commercial districts; San Diego, Portland, St. Louis, and Sacramento are just a few examples. Respecting the styles and methods of the past helps a city keep its personality. In a world where space and resources are limited, reusing old buildings is also a more sustainable, environmentally friendly, and practical alternative to the usual model of raze and rebuild.

In keeping with typical late-nineteenth- and early-twentieth-century patterns, the railroad built and rebuilt the depot at its same dominant position at the center of town even as other railroad facilities were moved toward the outskirts. Keeping passenger buildings in the center of town, rather than moving them farther east along with the maintenance yards and eventually the freight operations, ensured that railroad activities would continue to dominate the heart of the urban center. While this was good for the railroad, it posed obvious problems for the people living and working downtown.

### RAILROAD CROSSINGS

During Reno's early years there was only one major downtown rail crossing, at Sierra Street. Virginia Street and Center Street were blocked by Central Pacific's massive freight sheds, which stretched east-west for several blocks on the north side of the tracks. The Virginia & Truckee railroad tracks diverged from the main track in the middle of downtown as well, ran parallel to its south side, and then curved southward down Peavine Street (now Evans Avenue). Crossing the multiple sets of railroad tracks that split Reno in half was a daunting proposition for vehicles and pedestrians.

The city and the railroad began addressing pedestrian safety before dealing with the risks posed by increasing wagon and automobile traffic. There was no good way for pedestrians to get from the southern commercial side of the city to the northern residential side without negotiating five or more sets of active tracks. Passenger and freight trains passed through in both directions on the main lines, and freight cars were being stored, loaded, unloaded, and moved at all times of the day. Railroad personnel doubtless did not want the extra worry of members of the public wandering in and around the dangerous equipment.

Residents and city officials offered numerous proposals for downtown crossings around the turn of the century. One report from March 1902 suggests that the railroad had a plan for such a crossing. It proposed downward-sloping ramps that paralleled the rails on either side and then turned at right angles to cross under the tracks.[28] That plan was not enacted. The successful proposal, put to Southern Pacific president Edward H. Harriman on 23 May 1902 by a delegation of Reno businessmen, called for a tunnel under the tracks at Virginia Street. Harriman agreed that it was a good idea, a contract for six thousand dollars was negotiated between the city and the railroad on 17 October, and railroad crews were at work on the Virginia Street pedestrian subway by early November.[29]

Twelve men and two teams of horses or mules worked on the initial excavation under the tracks. The *Reno Evening Gazette* reported that a steam shovel was also used to good effect during the excavations.[30] The railroad's plans called for a concrete subway tunnel eight feet wide and eight feet high, with a wooden entry/exit kiosk with stairwells at each end. A bridge crew of ten men built vertical timber piles with caps to support the railroad during construction, and trains continued to run over the excavation on this makeshift trestle for the duration of the work. Although they had anticipated soils consisting of gravel and large boulders, the crews instead encountered fine brick clay, which made the work considerably easier. A strike delayed the project briefly when the twelve-man crew of Italian excavators demanded a pay raise from $1.60 to $2.00 a day. Their foreman ordered the ten better-paid carpenters building the trestle to take the laborers' places, but they refused and also walked off the job. The excavation crew returned to work the next day even though Southern Pacific refused to grant the raise.[31]

The north end kiosk came straight off the tunnel, but the south end kiosk was situated perpendicular to the tunnel, oriented east–west across Virginia Street. Southern Pacific probably chose to orient the kiosk across the street at least partly to discourage aboveground grade crossings there. When the city constructed a grade crossing at Virginia Street in 1913, the kiosk had to be realigned 180 degrees and moved out of the road.[32] The underpass was essentially finished by the end of 1902 and was open by January 1903.

Unflattering news reports about the subway surfaced almost immediately. The first incident appears to have occurred even before construction was completed, when a judge out for a nighttime stroll fell into the

The southern (*right center*) and northern (*lower left corner*) Virginia Street subway kiosks, ca. 1906. Note the pedestrians crossing the tracks. Courtesy of the Nevada Historical Society.

south stairwell and was slightly injured.[33] By late January and early February 1903, less than a month after it opened, the subway had sprung severe leaks; officials closed it at least three times that year for repairs.[34] The railroad crews were probably accustomed to building structures mainly for strength rather than for aesthetics or ease of use, and they seem to have made no provision for drainage. It is difficult to see how any could have been made, however, since the bottom of the tunnel was one of the deepest structures in town. The train tracks are only a few city blocks north of the Truckee River, and the water table in the area is notoriously high. Sitting fifteen feet below the ground surface, the tunnel would inevitably have gotten wet, if not flooded, during wet weather. A 1903 *Nevada State Journal* story relates the woeful tale of one George W. Perkins:

*Suffered a Shock*

Yesterday morning G. W. Perkins had occasion to cross the railroad track, and instead of going through the mud and slush wisely concluded that the subway was about the proper [*sic*]

Well, George started down the steps of the tunnel and had just gone a short distance when he met a lady that had started from the other side. The lady had encountered the big pond of water and had waded through it, and from the position she held her skirts it is thought that she anticipated wading through another.

Mr. Perkins gave one glance, and then, thinking discretion the better part of valor, attempted to flee. He slipped, then slid, then skated a little, and at last reports had reached home and was taking an inventory of himself.

As a usual thing Mr. Perkins is the essence of gallantry, but on this occasion he was taken so much by surprise that the only thing he thought of was home, sweet home.[35]

The *Journal* printed a joke about the subway the next month: "A young lady remarked to her fair companion, 'The man I marry must be willing to go through fire and water for me.' Her companion replied, 'You must mean by that he drink Reno whisky and walk through the subway on a rainy day.' "[36]

The other major problem with the tunnel was intrinsic: it was a subterranean public space in the middle of downtown, and it almost immediately began to attract vagrants and petty thieves who preyed on passersby. Reports of vandalism, robbery, and assault dominated news stories about the subway throughout its life span. Problems with lighting began immediately and continued throughout 1903, when someone repeatedly stole the subway's lightbulbs.[37] The lack of good lighting exacerbated the problems with criminals in the tunnel. Reno already had a reputation as a haven for drunks, vagrants, and thieves, and it is thus not surprising that locals perceived the subway as a magnet for unsavory elements. The city passed an ordinance in 1902 prohibiting writing or inscribing on the walls of the subway, and another in 1905 prohibiting loitering, loafing, congregating, or sitting in or about the subway.[38] In 1905 the city stationed a police officer to keep watch on the underpass but was neither willing nor able to pay for the position indefinitely.[39]

Apparently, enough people used the subway to make its maintenance worthwhile, however, as the city periodically continued to replace the lightbulbs. There is also some evidence that Reno citizens saw the area around the south entrance to the subway as a convenient central meeting point. In 1906 someone suggested placing a bandstand on top of the south kiosk at the north end of Virginia Street for open-air band concerts. Southern Pacific was quick to quash this idea, pointing out that the spectators would be standing on the tracks and that fast trains were likely to be passing through during concerts.[40] In 1907 the city decided to take advantage of the site's popularity and began posting legal notices on the south kiosk in a spot where citizens were likely to see them. Plans to place a fountain at the south entrance came to naught.[41]

Crossing the multiple sets of tracks above the ground continued to be dangerous. In 1912 a train hit and killed a young teacher named Gertrude O'Hara as she crossed the tracks at Sierra Street.[42] She did not notice an eastbound train approaching because the noise from a westbound train drowned out its approach. There were at least five sets of tracks through this area, and multiple trains often passed at the same time. After describing the accident in gory detail, the *Reno Evening Gazette* emphasized the ongoing danger at grade crossings by listing several other recent accidents and noting: "The Sierra street crossing is the busiest in the city, being even busier than the Lake street crossing, but still it is unprotected by automatic gates."[43]

After lengthy agitation by local officials, a lookout tower and manually controlled crossing gate were installed at Sierra Street later in 1912. Operators occupied the towers during the daytime, but the city and the railroad could not agree whether or how nighttime operation should be funded.[44]

For a year, Southern Pacific resisted the city's demands to extend other downtown streets across the tracks. In 1913 the city won out and extended Virginia Street across the tracks. Safety structures similar to those at Sierra Street were installed, and operators in the Sierra Street tower also controlled the new Virginia Street gates.[45] The city evidently still considered the underpass useful enough to merit realigning both entryway kiosks out of the street and extensively remodeling them. The new kiosks were built of steel, stucco, and concrete in the Mission style and boasted new Mission-style lighting.[46] Once the Virginia Street grade crossing was completed, pedestrians could cross the tracks more safely and there was less need for a pedestrian subway; its use declined. During the 1918 influenza epidemic, rumors flew that the subway was a source of the disease.[47] Few people ventured into it after that.

The large freight sheds that dominated the downtown landscape blocked another main north-south street, Center. Local newspapers editorialized on the need to remove the sheds as early as 1907 and continued their efforts almost every year afterward until the sheds were ultimately removed. A 1907 *Nevada State Journal* editorial about the sheds reflects the railroad's influence on the development of Reno: "To maintain the sheds where they now are, is seriously to interfere with the growth of Reno. . . . It prevents the development of the north side of the city, as anyone can see. [Center Street] is the street on which the main entrance to the University opens, and it is the most direct road to that institution, but anyone leaving the train must make a detour of what amounts to two blocks to reach the street."[48] By 1929 some of the editorials had become

*Top:* Overview of downtown Reno, 1920. The Center Street freight sheds are visible in the center. Courtesy of the Nevada Historical Society.

*Bottom:* View north down Center Street toward the freight sheds, ca. 1915. Courtesy of the Nevada Historical Society.

more strident; one from the *Journal* employs a tone common to local journalistic criticisms of the railroad company:

> Promises are easily made. It is less difficult to make them than it is to carry them out. But when an institution as big as the Southern Pacific Company makes a promise it is safe to assume that the promise will be fulfilled. Reno business men and organizations . . . have been looking forward faithfully to the Southern Pacific Company's promise to remove the freight sheds from their present location to another along the tracks several blocks west. But as yet nothing has been done about it.[49]

As Reno's number of annual visitors, local population, and economic profits increased, the city gained the leverage it needed to open the Center Street thoroughfare against the wishes of the railroad. Southern Pacific finally conceded in 1931 and built new freight sheds east of Lake Street for its operations, removing the Center Street sheds and placing crossing signals at the new grade crossing. For the first time, Reno's business district was free to expand on both sides of the railroad tracks. Commercial development on the north side of the tracks increased with the improved access, and Reno's economy grew as a result. The 1931 opening of Center Street coincided with the lifting of the 1910 gambling ban and the shortening of the residency requirement for divorce to six weeks.[50]

Southern Pacific installed additional hand-operated crossing signals at Lake Street, Chestnut (Arlington) Street, and other grade crossings over the years. Automatic gates were not installed until 1956, when Southern Pacific placed them at Lake, Center, Sierra, and Virginia streets.[51]

The ReTRAC project uncovered three signal-related sites. A series of wooden conduits was found to run both parallel and perpendicular to the railroad tracks in eleven different locations on one of these sites. Each conduit consisted of a wooden timber with a channel cut into it, capped with a board. The channels contained rubber-wrapped copper wires—some of which had been later repaired with modern synthetic insulation material—related to railroad signal and track-switching electrical systems. The channels were most likely installed in the late nineteenth century, when the use of this type of wooden conduit was most common.

The second signal-related site was a rectangular terra cotta conduit running within a V-shaped wooden channel. The use of wooden conduit in combination with terra cotta conduit was unique in the project area, and the date and function of this conduit are unknown.

The foundation and part of the upright post for a railroad semaphore that was part of the railroad's internal signaling system was uncovered under Third Street, just west of Virginia Street. The concrete-encased upright consisted of two steel casings, one inside the other; both had been cut off with a torch at or just below the modern ground surface. As a railroad semaphore base, this feature was most likely in use between 1875 and 1920.

Semaphores, so named for their resemblance to semaphore flags, were a crucial component of the electric signaling system that informed train operators whether they could proceed and with how much caution. The system was born in 1872 when William Robinson patented the electric closed-track circuit. An approaching train or a rail break would interrupt an electric current traveling through the rails in a block of track, generating a signal. The electric closed-track circuit was in turn part of the automatic block signal system, which maintained a fixed minimum interval of space between any two trains traveling on the same track in the same direction.[52]

The early manifestation of this signaling system used electrical components but still relied on telegraphic communication. The mechanically operated semaphore signals employed a wire cable connected to a tower staffed by a signalman (sometimes some distance away). The arm on the semaphore's post could be moved from a vertical position to a horizontal position to indicate "go" or "stop"; railroads widely adopted these signals, along with an intermediate position indicating "proceed with caution," after 1908.

In the early twentieth century, wholly electrical automatic signaling systems came into use, reducing the need for manned interlocking towers. Some railroads continued to use automatic block signaling systems using telegraph or telephone and mechanical signals, especially on small, single-track lines.[53] Improvements in electrical systems, especially the increased availability of alternating current, enabled the replacement of semaphores with light signals. The new signals were better suited to situations of poor visibility and had no mechanical components, which were prone to failure.[54] In 1923 the number of light signals exceeded the number of semaphores for the first time.[55] A 1926 *Reno Evening Gazette* article bemoans the semaphore's decline: "The railroad semaphore, whose familiar lines have stood out so long against the sky in metropolis and tank town, is giving way to the march of industrial progress."[56]

Southern Pacific began replacing all of its remaining semaphores in 1905 when, the *Nevada State Journal* noted, it "decided to install electric block signals to the exclusion of all others" throughout its system.[57] This article does not specifically mention the Reno railroad segment as one of those in which the replacement would take place, suggesting that Reno was not topmost on the list of locations meriting new equipment. A historical photo of the Reno railroad corridor taken about 1915 shows semaphores still in use at that time.[58] The semaphore base buried under Third Street probably functioned until 1915–20.

As aboveground traffic increased, the pedestrian subway languished, rarely used. The city council recommended its closing in June 1923,[59] but the recommendation was not enacted until four years later because the railroad objected, most likely for liability reasons. Southern Pacific wanted to be able to point to the available safe underground passageway if someone were injured crossing the tracks above ground. Apparently the city had the final say, and the tunnel was boarded up on orders from the city council in October 1927.[60]

The tunnel and the entrance kiosks were reused for unrelated purposes for years afterward. In 1928 the city leased the north kiosk to the Nevada Transit Company, operator of bus services between Reno and Sparks, as a ticket station.[61] In 1930 the railroad installed a boiler in the south kiosk to heat private railway cars parked there during cold weather; the boiler was removed in the late 1940s.[62] In 1932 service station operator Herman Baker contracted with the city to use the tunnel as a storage area for tires and other automotive parts.[63] The subway's demise finally came in February 1957, when the city council gave the property back to Southern Pacific for demolition of the southern kiosk. The newspaper article recounting this action notes that the northern kiosk had already been covered over.[64] Southern Pacific tore down the southern kiosk in July 1957, and the *Nevada State Journal* rejoiced in the removal of "an unsightly mark on the landscape."[65]

Archaeological investigations showed that although the surface kiosk had been demolished, most of the underground portions of the pedestrian underpass were merely filled in and forgotten. Extensive testing with a small backhoe conducted under the sidewalk on the west side of Virginia Street just south of the tracks verified the location of the subway and confirmed that it was still intact. In fact, modern utility crews had run lines through the tunnel, using it as a convenient conduit. The test-

Cross section of the pedestrian subway, with the wooden posts of the 1902 temporary trestle visible on either side. Courtesy of WCRM, Inc.

ing also exposed fragmentary remnants of the temporary wooden trestle on which the trains ran during the original 1902 excavations for the tunnel. A sample core of the concrete tunnel's eastern wall showed it to be about three feet thick.

A utility line excavation later in the project exposed the underground portion of the subway's southern entry kiosk. The concrete structure, containing two stairwells and their connecting horizontal landing, was still intact and still connected to the main tunnel. Judging by its location and orientation, this underground entrance to the subway was built in 1913 as part of the kiosk realignment out of the newly opened Virginia Street.

The final exposure of the subway occurred during excavation of the main train trench, which uncovered almost the entire length of the tunnel structure. After recording the tunnel in place, archaeologists monitored heavy equipment as operators cut the tunnel in half.

The tunnel's cross section showed that it had been built in three stages. The floor was laid, then the walls were raised, and finally the roof was poured around three parallel metal reinforcements running across the tunnel's top. These reinforcements were recycled scrap rail, approximately 50 pounds per yard in gauge. This was by far the lightest rail found on sites during the ReTRAC project and may represent some of the earliest rail used on the transcontinental railroad. Central Pacific Railroad is reported to have used 56-pound rail on the original transcontinental line.[66] Modern rail weighs about 135 pounds per yard or more, and rails from the turn of the century were already up to about 75–90 pounds per yard. This use of old scrap rail for subway reinforcement confirms the historical accounts that the railroad constructed the subway. The method of concrete pour construction left gaps between the tunnel's parts that would have contributed to the water leakage problems. It is clear that railroad sensibilities prevailed with regard to design and construction methods as well. The subway was overbuilt for assured stability and underengineered for actual human use.

## COMMERCE AND THE RAILROAD

The layout of Reno's commercial district is another key element in reading the city's landscape. The commercial and industrial district has always been oriented to the main line railroad corridor and has depended on easy accessibility to shipping by rail. The downtown core originally had businesses oriented toward providing goods and services both to locals and to rail passengers stopping in town; the Commercial Row area was dominated by saloons, restaurants, hotels, retail stores, and services such as banks and barbershops. Later, large gambling establishments came to dominate downtown. The areas farther east and west of downtown leaned more to the industrial side and were dominated by larger-scale endeavors such as warehouses, lumber yards, breweries, bottling works, concrete manufacturers, and meatpacking plants.

Commercial development was centered on Commercial Row until the early twentieth century, when the business district's slow southward expansion down Virginia Street began to accelerate. The large casino operations established after World War II moved gambling away from small back-alley locations and onto Virginia. In 1947 Reno restricted casino gambling to a commercial district centered on Virginia Street, with a "red line" drawn around it. Casino owners tested and pushed the boundaries of the district throughout the 1950s, and in the late 1960s the city opened gambling to outside interests and allowed casinos outside the red line area. The Red Line Ordinance was formally removed in 1970. Downtown's commercial district quickly expanded north across the railroad tracks as large hotel-casinos tried to monopolize tourist traffic as it exited from Interstate 80, before it could reach the older businesses to the south.

While Reno's downtown business district has changed drastically since the nineteenth century, the industrial districts outside the downtown core have largely maintained their old pattern. Much of the industrial district still occupies land owned by the railroad, now Union Pacific. Both historical and modern businesses have leased right-of-way property from the railroad and have heavily utilized spurs of the main line for moving raw materials and finished products. The construction dates of most of the short, localized track offshoots recorded during the ReTRAC project suggest a particularly active period of spur placement to private businesses leasing railroad property between 1906 and 1918. This period of activity corresponds to a general pre–World War I increase in commercial and industrial enterprise in the areas east and west of the main downtown business district, and reflects the continued influence of railroad landscapes on the physical establishment of commercial enterprise in Reno.

The commercial building vestiges recorded during the ReTRAC project include lumber and building material companies, bottling works, wholesale meat and produce warehouses, a grocery and hardware store, equipment supply companies, automobile service stations, and one of downtown's first parking garages. One typical site consisted of concrete foundation vestiges of commercial/industrial buildings constructed between 1918 and 1921 that primarily housed produce wholesalers until the mid-1930s. These warehouse and distribution operations are typical of the types of large-scale commercial enterprises that used railroad spurs for receiving and shipping purposes, mostly in the area east of the main downtown core.

Among the commercial structural vestiges was a buried concrete wall remnant running roughly east–west north of the main line railroad tracks. Research proved it was part of a "pigeonhole" parking structure constructed by Harolds Club in 1953–54. Harolds Club, which was established in 1936, was downtown's most dominant casino enterprise at the time of its construction and continued to be influential into the early 1980s. To alleviate growing parking problems downtown, Harolds Club hired the Pigeonhole Parking Company to construct a six-tier parking garage at an estimated cost of $300,000.[67] The concept of pigeonhole, or "stackable," parking structures dates to at least 1921. These structures use elevators, rather than ramps, to move vehicles to individual parking spaces. This is a space-saving alternative to conventional parking structures, requiring less than two-thirds of their area and half of their volume. By 1960, ownership of the pigeonhole parking garage had passed from Harolds Club to McFarland's Flying A Service and was associated with the service station nearby. The garage was demolished after 1972.

One of the oldest commercial building vestiges found was a previously unrecorded component of Reno's oldest standing commercial building, the Masonic Hall, at the corner of Commercial Row and Sierra Street.

Masonic Hall sidewalk vault. Courtesy of WCRM, Inc.

The removal of sidewalk concrete for construction of a power pole component on Sierra exposed a linear block of three basement rooms. The rooms lie directly under the sidewalk, beyond the surface footprint of the building. Sidewalk basements, also known as sidewalk vaults, were a common type of storage in nineteenth-century buildings. The main room running the length of the building is about eighty-five feet long by ten feet wide, and its ceiling is made up of a series of concrete barrel vaults lined with brick. The vaults are supported by a series of six-inch-diameter iron pillars, each standing in a narrow concrete pad, running the length of the room. According to the owners of the building at the time of the excavation (Fitzgerald's Casino), these pillars were installed in the late 1980s to keep the roof from collapsing during the installation of paving stones on downtown sidewalks.[68] The east wall of the room, which is part of the building's foundation, is composed of cobbles, boulders, and rough-cut stones set in mortar. The entrance to the rooms lies to the south via metal-clad double doors leading from the main building basement. The doorway through the stone foundation wall is lined with brick and has an arched brick lintel.

Local builder Septimus F. Hoole constructed the Reno Masonic Hall in 1872, and its grand opening took place on 21 February 1873. The local chapter of the Masonic Lodge met in a large, secured room at the front of the building's second floor. The ground floor served as a grocery and hardware store, under a series of owners, until 1970. James C. Hagerman owned and operated the first grocery and hardware store on the first floor from 1873 to 1883; between 1879 and 1883 Jerry Schooling partnered with Hagerman in the endeavor. The basement of the building, which was used for storage of grocery and hardware goods, has mortared boulder and cobble foundation walls and was part of the original construction.

In 1881 Hagerman and Schooling added a twenty-five-foot addition to the rear of the building. The addition matches the rest of the structure in style and materials and contributes to its significance. It is possible that the owners installed the three basement rooms at the time of this addition, as they do not appear to be an original part of the main basement structure to the east. An August 1881 *Reno Evening Gazette* article confirms that some excavation work was done during construction of the addition: "The foundation and cellar for the addition to the Masonic building is completed and the brick work has already made quite a showing."[69] The sidewalk vault may be related to this "foundation and cellar." No other major additions are known, and renovations consisted of exterior features such as canopies and front windows. Gallatin and Folsom operated the business from 1883 to 1895, and the Reno Mercantile Company ran it from 1895 to 1970; it is likely that all of the mercantiles used the narrow sidewalk vault as storage space, accessing it directly through the sidewalk via steel doors.

The building appears to have had another sidewalk vault on its north side, at the main entrance on Commercial Row. Photographs from circa 1910 show horse-drawn wagons in front of open doors in that sidewalk and goods being loaded or unloaded directly into or out of basements. The north wall of the Masonic building's basement exhibits a corresponding bricked-up opening that once would have connected the Commercial Row sidewalk vault with the main basement. Many nineteenth-century sidewalk vaults were partially illuminated by glass prisms set directly into the sidewalk, and close examination of the front entryway of the Masonic building revealed a few prisms still set in the sidewalk, covered with years of grime.

We discovered only one exclusively residential-related historical site during the ReTRAC project, and that was a trash scatter containing such household items as ceramics, beverage bottles (both alcoholic and nonalcoholic), patent medicine bottles, ink bottles, bones of butchered animals, and bisque doll parts. This site was located right next to the main line railroad tracks and was not associated with building remnants or other features. It illustrates another function of the railroad corridor: expedient trash disposal for nearby households. In the days before municipal trash pickup, residents disposed of their own refuse wherever they could and may well have found the open space of the railroad corridor convenient for dumping. Public but not picturesque, the right-of-way probably would have ended up with railroad detritus too. This area, located a short distance before the Reno stop, would have been a handy place for trains to dispose of garbage that accumulated during the run from Oakland/Sacramento to Reno. The high number of sites related to commercial occupations versus residential occupations reflects the way development was oriented both physically and economically around the railroad corridor.

THE TWENTIETH CENTURY was a time of great change for the railroad industry. The rise of the automobile led to legislation supporting and regularizing highway programs across the nation, and the railroads no longer had a virtual monopoly on public travel. By 1970 the nation's passenger railways were in such bad financial shape that individual rail companies turned intercity rail passenger traffic over to the federally subsidized Amtrak. The changing nature of the railroads had a concomitant effect on Reno. With more freight and visitors arriving by truck and car, respectively, than by train, proximity to the train station was no longer as important for either tourist-oriented businesses or industrial companies receiving or shipping goods. The importance of downtown passenger and freight depots declined at the same time. Owners demolished some of the buildings, such as the Southern Pacific freight sheds, and sold others, including the American Railway Express Depot and the Nevada-California-Oregon Depot, to be used in other ways, reflecting yet another facet of downtown's changing use patterns.

Although the railroad retains ownership of the transcontinental right-of-way corridor through the heart of town, over the years it has had to contend with the demands accompanying Reno's development into a major urban center. Negotiations, often intense, between the railroad and the city resulted in changes to the city's urban infrastructure, most notably the opening of downtown streets across the tracks to create better north-south access, the placement of safety signals and crossing gates, and the joint funding and construction of the Virginia Street pedestrian underpass. The city's commercial district changed along with the railroad, eventually expanding well beyond the original core. All of these developments combined to produce Reno's urban landscape, and when this landscape is viewed within the economic, political, and social context of the city-railroad relationship, the ties between the two entities are clear. Other aspects of Reno's infrastructure system developed in different ways but are equally readable in the modern urban landscape.

CHAPTER

4

# City Infrastructure and Everyday Life

The presence of infrastructure systems—the basic services and facilities that enable a community to function—is a hallmark of urban centers. Communications networks, power lines, water conveyance systems, and transportation networks comprise the circulatory system of a city and enable large numbers of people to live in an area without overwhelming the available space and natural resources. Without a working infrastructure, an urban center has trouble functioning; this is evident after any natural disaster. The archaeological remains of sewer vaults, water pipes, and cisterns are not exactly glamorous, but they offer a great deal of information about the day-to-day life of Reno's past residents.

We recorded the remnants of many historical infrastructure-related features during the ReTRAC project. In addition to the more complete sites described below, the discoveries included numerous remnants of indeterminate age and association; most were small pipe fragments. Municipal systems—water, sewer, electric, and so on—tend to require frequent repairs; the improvement of old services and replacement with new materials and alignments over the years have destroyed many of Reno's historical utilities. The transitions between different iterations of municipal systems are thus often difficult to discern archaeologically. Furthermore, utility networks are preserved to different extents in different parts of town; some areas have been highly disturbed by modern work, others less so. Most of Reno has seen significant disturbance from underground construction, maintenance, and repair, leaving somewhat spotty evidence of infrastructure features in the town's various geographical areas. Research into the surviving intact features using historical maps and other archival sources is still possible, however. These mundane sites can provide information about urban planning, spatial organization, municipal services, and the general quality of life in an urban environment. Studying the ways in which utility systems develop over time and across geographic space can also help to trace the physical and social development of a community.

Although Central Pacific carefully planned and platted Reno's townsite, it paid less attention to the settlement's infrastructure. During the late nineteenth and early twentieth centuries, the community experienced relatively rapid economic and population growth. It became clear that the developing city needed a centralized way to provide for its residents' needs: clean water, trash disposal, sewage management, telephone services, gas lighting and heating, electricity, and railroad crossings. Unlike its streets and blocks, Reno's water, sewer, gas, and electric systems grew in response to dire needs rather than in anticipation of them. This was partly because Reno did not incorporate as a town until 1903; prior to that, Washoe County resolved pressing problems. Because Reno was the county's population center, the county commissioners were quite responsive to its needs, albeit sometimes only after goading by downtown business owners. But the lack of a mayor and city council deprived Reno of a strong voice when it came to dealing with powerful corporations.

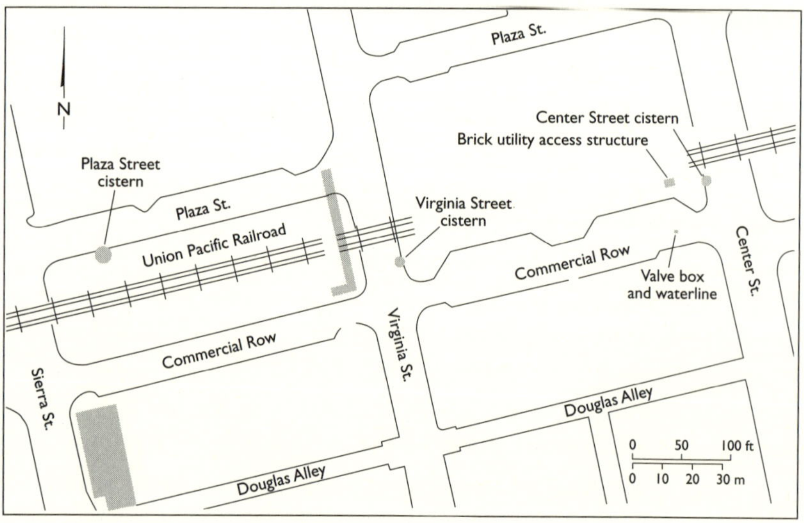


Streets and locations of sites discussed in this chapter.

Incorporation actually followed establishment of most of the fundamental elements of an urban infrastructure system, including a water supply and a primitive sewage disposal network. The water system in particular played a key role in the eventual incorporation of the town and in the organization of the early city government. Predictably, utilities were developed first in the downtown core, where the business district was centered and where the late-nineteenth-century occupation rate was highest, and then spread outward into the residential and industrial districts on the outskirts of town. The process was neither orderly nor smooth.

## FIRE CISTERNS

Fire cisterns were the first elements to be put into place, prompted by several fires in downtown Reno during the late 1860s and early 1870s. The first fire of note occurred in 1868, when a discarded cigar set a stable ablaze. This fire, small though it was, inspired the town to organize an informal volunteer fire department; the agreement was that all able-bodied men would help in the event of a fire.

The town's first major conflagration occurred in October 1873, when a fire that started in the Western Hotel spread to neighboring buildings and destroyed about one hundred structures along Commercial Row. Neighboring Truckee, Wadsworth, and (belatedly) Carson City sent their fire engines, but the fire consumed most of the buildings on Commercial Row to the east and west of Virginia Street before firefighters could stop it.[1] The *Nevada State Journal* was optimistic that the town would recover: "Right here however we desire to state that Reno will arise Phoenix like and be better and brighter than ever before. The businessmen of Reno are good, true men. They are men of energy, ability and though they may not all be men of capital, they have that which will make capital—hard muscles and a spirit that knows no such word as fail."[2]

Five downtown commercial buildings burned in 1875; later that year, Reno organized a fire department. The following year the town purchased a hand engine from Gold Hill and a pumper from New York. The arrival of the new pumper was cause for an impromptu parade through downtown led by the Reno Brass Band.[3] One month later the fire department built an engine house on Plaza Street, just north of the railroad tracks; it had two stories and a wooden walkway to the Plaza Street cistern.

In 1877 the topmost story of the three-story Depot Hotel went up in flames, killing chambermaid Lena Johnson. Although some secondary accounts state that the Depot Hotel burned to the ground in that fire, primary accounts indicate that only the third floor and attic burned; the rest of the building survived, albeit with severe water damage that necessitated major repairs.[4] In 1878 Reno's Chinatown, located on both sides of First Street between Virginia and Center, burned to the ground; its residents relocated to the Lake Street area.

Reno's best-known disaster occurred on 2 March 1879 when strong winds spread sparks from a building's chimney to a stack of firewood, then fanned the flames to adjoining buildings. The water in the cisterns was quickly exhausted and the fire went on to destroy about 350 buildings, brick and masonry structures as well as wooden ones. Six people died in the conflagration. This death toll would not be exceeded until 2006, when twelve died in the Mizpah Hotel fire. At the time of the 1879 fire, however, the *Reno Evening Gazette* could imagine no worse disaster: "No report could portray the BLACK MISERY and heavy despair which now rests upon us. The beautiful little city which saw the sun rise in the morning sat at noon in the ashes stretching her scorched arms to heaven in prayers for help. For six long hours the boiling flames fed upon her vitals, eating her limbs and drinking her blood while her citizens looked helplessly on or indulged in unavailing struggles to stay the destroying element."[5]

The fire burned and warped a mile-long section of the railroad tracks, but crews working around the clock repaired it within two days.[6] With the remains of downtown still smoldering, cleanup and rebuilding began the very next day, and merchants proffered goods rescued from the flames. Many of the town's businesses took the opportunity to relocate to Virginia Street, farther away from the chaos of the railroad yards immediately adjacent to Commercial Row.

The last major nineteenth-century fire downtown occurred in May 1889, when the Nevada Theater at the corner of Center Street and Commercial Row caught on fire. The blaze spread west and east, destroying the Depot Hotel and eventually leveling an entire city block. After this fire Reno took steps to organize and provision a professional, full-time fire department. By 1893 the community had provided funds for clothing and a salaried position for an engine driver; in 1899 it funded three more firefighter positions. By 1904 all of Reno's firefighters were full-time

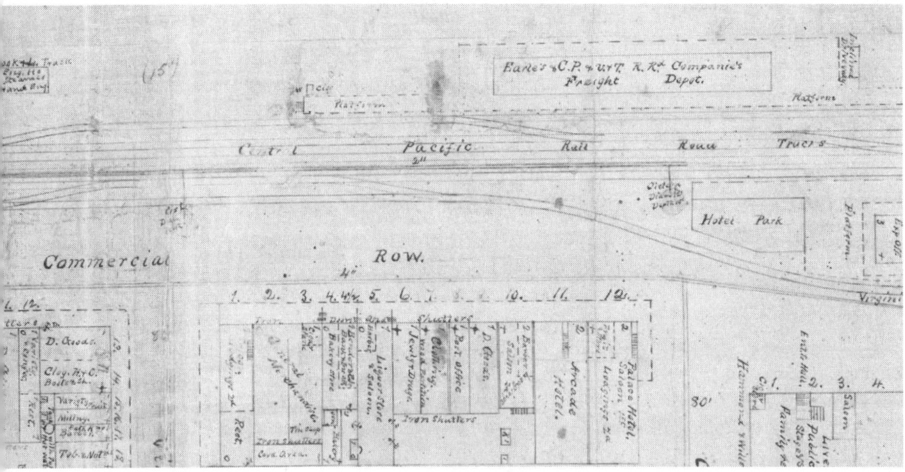


Reno's first cisterns, shown as circles at the north ends of Center Street (*right*) and Virginia Street (*left*), on an 1879 map. Courtesy of the Nevada Historical Society.

employees based at a large brick fire station at the corner of West Street and Commercial Row.[7] Downtown fires continued through the twentieth century, causing varying amounts of physical damage and sometimes taking lives.

We located and excavated Reno's first two underground cisterns, built between 1868 and 1874 in response to the autumn 1868 fire.[8] The Center Street cistern was associated with the Depot Hotel and lies under the western portion of Center Street, south of the main line tracks and north of the Virginia & Truckee tracks. The Virginia Street cistern lies under the eastern portion of Virginia Street, south of the main line tracks and north of Commercial Row. Both cisterns remain intact and were not altered or removed during the ReTRAC project.

The cisterns are circular brick structures built into the ground and lined with cement. Newspaper articles from the period indicate that each held approximately 10,000 gallons of water.[9] The archaeological excavation of the cisterns revealed that each cistern actually would have held more than 13,000 gallons when filled to capacity. The cisterns were capped with wooden covers that could be removed when water was needed to fight fires. Firefighters drew water from the cisterns using hand-pumped engines and, later, a steam engine.

At least two cisterns were in place when the fire of October 1873 occurred. A *Nevada State Journal* article notes, however, that "by the time buckets were brought out, cisterns uncovered, etc. the flames had spread with such rapidity that the entire vicinity was one burning mass."[10] While it is presumed that this article refers to the underground brick cisterns, it may also refer to smaller surface cisterns, which would have been large wooden barrels. Such cisterns were common during that period. The Virginia Street cistern was not one of the two in place for the 1873 fire, as an 1874 *Journal* article notes: "Work has been commenced on the cistern at the head of Virginia Street. It will be completed shortly, when the residents along Commercial Row may feel a little more safety, should a fire occur."[11]

The community built a third downtown cistern, north of the main line tracks, in the summer of 1876. The *Reno Evening Gazette* reported the good news: "Workmen are engaged in digging a cistern near the railroad track, at the intersection of Sierra and Plaza streets. The cistern will be seventeen feet in diameter by eight feet in depth on the inside, and will consequently hold nearly 13,000 gallons of water. . . . With this cistern in such a central location, and the 1400 feet of hose, the fire companies can reach a conflagration in the main business portion of the city."[12] A *Gazette* article from October 1876 implies that there was some grumbling about it from nearby property owners: "The cistern on Plaza street paid for itself Thursday morning, and probably made certain property holders ashamed of their conduct in regard to its construction."[13] Before Reno was incorporated in 1903, residents expected downtown's private business owners to help pay for municipal improvements such as cisterns, and presumably for sidewalks and boardwalks, street improvements, and lighting as well. The specific property owners to whom the *Gazette* so pointedly refers are unknown.

The Plaza Street cistern was at the center of downtown's firefighting infrastructure. A wooden walkway connected it to the small wooden fire engine house, enabling easy access for pump engines. It was the only one of the three downtown cisterns actually used during the fire that leveled most of Reno on 2 March 1879; the other two were inaccessible because of the flames.[14] Given the strength of the winds and the flammable nature of almost everything in town, however, it is unlikely that the equipment of the day could have stopped the fire even with unlimited water.

Reno built a number of other cisterns over the years, both downtown and later in residential districts as these grew larger and more densely populated. A report from the secretary of the fire department indicates that workers constructed six cisterns and a fire hydrant between March

1882 and March 1883 alone.[15] Each cistern was either six feet deep and six feet in diameter, or eight feet deep and eight feet in diameter. According to the report, the smaller ones had a capacity of about 1,270 gallons each and the larger ones about 3,015 gallons—all much smaller than the 13,000-plus gallon capacity of the 1870s cisterns. Not all of them were constructed of brick and cement: an 1882 newspaper article notes the completion of a subsurface cistern built of redwood at the corner of West and Second streets.[16]

The archaeological remains of the Center Street, Virginia Street, and Plaza Street cisterns indicate that they were nearly identical in construction style, size, and water capacity. All three had an interior diameter of seventeen feet and were seven and a half to eight feet deep; structures of this size would have had a capacity of approximately 13,600 gallons of water. Remnants of a wooden cover survived only on the top of the Center Street cistern, but all of the cisterns are presumed to have had wooden covers. The cisterns' interior walls were tooled cement over brick; their exteriors were bounded by a layer of clay that probably assisted in water retention. The pattern in which the bricks were laid was nearly identical on the three cisterns, with minor variations on the rims probably reflecting the work of different bricklayers. Overall, the standardized construction styles and sizes suggest that the three cisterns were part of an organized community firefighting system, not private structures belonging to the individual business owners who helped pay for their construction.

With improvements in Reno's water delivery system in the late 1880s, the fire department began switching from cisterns to hydrants. This appears to have been a gradual transition: excavation of the Virginia Street cistern revealed that a three-inch water line had been added to the cistern after its construction. The water line extended through a hole chipped through the brick wall and then sealed with mortar; it had a brass fill valve and would have facilitated filling and pumping of the cistern. The Plaza Street cistern is known to have had two three-inch water lines running to it in 1876,[17] and the Virginia Street cistern's water line may have had a similarly early placement date. Most of the cisterns apparently remained in use, or at least in reserve, until the early twentieth century. A number of newspaper accounts contain complaints about disrepair of the cisterns' wooden covers.[18] One cistern had been filled in and abandoned by January 1902; according to the *Nevada State Journal,* the Center Street cistern had been "rendered useless on account of the curbing along the edge of the pavement, preventing an engine getting close enough to take water."[19] The same article notes that hydrants had been placed on all existing water mains large enough to supply them, and on newly placed mains as needed. The Center Street and Virginia Street cisterns do not appear on Sanborn fire insurance maps after 1899 and were filled in and covered over between 1899 and 1904. The Plaza Street cistern appears on the 1906 Sanborn map but not the 1918 map, meaning that it was not fully abandoned until sometime between 1906 and 1918.

Each cistern was filled in with a different material. The Center Street cistern was filled with a homogeneous, unstratified deposit of mine waste rock, probably from one or more of the nearby mines on Peavine Mountain. This fill contained one datable diagnostic artifact: a knurled screw cap on a bottle finish dating to sometime after 1924. Although the artifact may indicate a later cistern fill date than is indicated by the disappearance of the feature from Sanborn fire insurance maps after 1899, it more likely represents later trash dumping into the abandoned cistern. Archaeological exploration exposed newer pipes that city utility workers had laid through the Center Street cistern over the years. Because the Center Street cistern was located in the rail yard in the center of town, it may not have been covered over permanently until Center Street was extended across the tracks in 1931.

The Virginia Street cistern was filled with rounded cobbles and small boulders of local origin. While this cistern was most likely filled in and abandoned between 1899 and 1904, it is possible that it was not permanently covered over until Virginia Street was extended across the tracks in 1913.

The Plaza Street cistern was filled with clay-rich, gravel-bearing sands. In 1905 Reno's fire chief recommended that this cistern on Plaza and Third streets be filled and abandoned.[20] Since this cistern disappeared from Sanborn fire insurance maps after 1906, it appears the fire chief's recommendation was followed.

## WATER CONVEYANCE SYSTEMS

The establishment of a reliable water conveyance system in Reno was a long and laborious process. The community's early residents drew their water directly from the Truckee River, from private wells, or from one of the twelve-plus ditches flowing through town. Like other Nevada towns, Reno's development was closely linked to its proximity to water and to

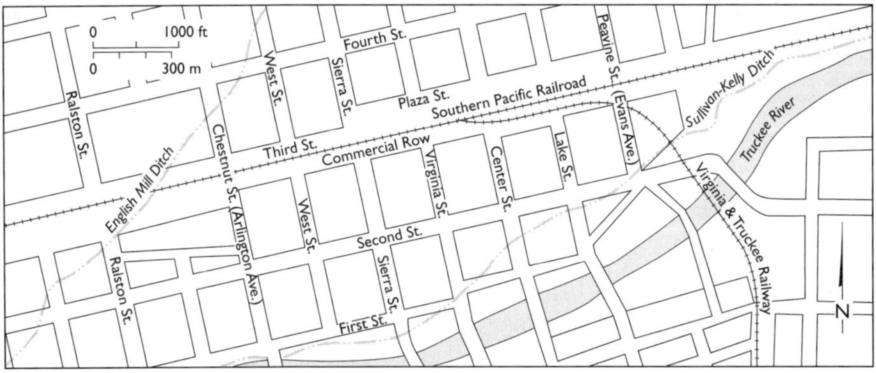


Routes of the English Mill and Sullivan-Kelly ditches through town, 1931. Based on a map from the City of Reno Engineering Department.

the establishment of water distribution and storage systems. Diversions for agricultural irrigation, logging transportation, early utilities, and milling helped shape the nature of the young city. Interests outside of and independent of Reno carried out many of these endeavors; though ditches and flumes built by private companies such as the Riverside Flour Mill or the Orr Ditch Company may have run through Reno, they were not originally part of the city infrastructure.

At least one of the area's prominent water conveyance features, the English Mill Ditch, predated the town itself. A mining and milling operation constructed the approximately four-mile-long ditch in 1865 in order to transport water from the Truckee River to the English Mill, an ore-processing facility for the mines on Peavine Mountain, northwest of town. Water from the ditch powered the mining operation's stamp mill, irrigated nearby agricultural areas, and ran a flour mill at the nearby company town of Auburn, Nevada.[21] Ditch construction reached its peak in the 1870s, when the Orr, Steamboat, Sullivan-Kelly, and Highland ditches were built.

Longtime Reno resident Harold Curran told us that people used ditch and flume water for drinking, washing, trash disposal, and recreation.[22] They also tried to use ditch water to fight fires downtown, but the limited number of pumps and the seasonal ebb in water volume rendered the ditches practically useless for that purpose. Bridges covered the ditches where they crossed streets and alleys downtown. Reno officials considered bridges part of the streets and alleys and repaired them even though the ditches were not owned by the city.[23]

As time went by, residents began to regard the ditches as dangerous nuisances. A disturbing number of newspaper articles document children drowning in the ditches and victims of foul play being dumped in them. In 1927 a group of mothers addressed a meeting of Reno's school parents' associations, voicing their concerns about the many open, swiftly flowing ditches running through town. This led to the formation of the United Parent-Teachers' Association, consolidating the schools' individual PTAs, but did not eliminate the ditches.[24] By 1941 at least fifteen children had died in the ditches, and the campaign to fence, cover over, and ultimately consolidate and eliminate many of the water channels continued.[25] During the next twenty-five years, some ditch owners turned their ditches over to the city, which put them to more urban usages such as flood control and drainage. By the early 1960s, workers had fenced or covered over and buried ditches that were still used for their original purpose, at least in the more congested parts of town.

Work along the railroad corridor uncovered several ditch sites. Excavations for a utilities realignment exposed two segments of the English Mill Ditch, one underneath Ralston Street and the other just to the east, where the ditch passed under the railroad tracks. The ditch was originally rock lined and measured approximately seven feet wide by four feet deep. At some point between 1910 and 1950, someone constructed a box

A segment of the English Mill Ditch running under the railroad grade. Courtesy of WCRM, Inc.

culvert-type concrete storm drain within the ditch's cobble-lined walls and covered over and buried the previously open ditch. The hardened silt sediments within the storm drain contained numerous artifacts; many of these were modern, but bottles dating to the 1930s were also present.

Several segments of the 1872 Sullivan-Kelly Ditch were found under the railroad tracks near Sutro Street in the eastern portion of the project area. The ditch was originally cobble lined, with a later concrete pour atop the cobbles. Its passage underneath the tracks was marked by two nearly identical concrete box culverts, one on either side of the railroad grade. Correspondence from the Reno Public Works Department indicates that some unspecified portions of the ditch were still in use in 1967, even after being covered.[26] The discovery of these ditches under the city streets evokes images of an earlier landscape in which irrigation channels carried water from the river all over the Truckee Meadows.

As Reno grew, so did the demand for a municipal water supply. In 1870–71 Smith Hill's Reno Water Company built a pipeline connecting to the Hunter Creek Ditch, which diverted water from year-round Hunter Creek in the foothills west of town.[27] The water company did not extend pipes outside the main part of town until 1874. The earliest pipes were made of wood or riveted iron of fairly small diameter, and were often shattered by winter freezes or by wagon traffic at busy intersections. The water company converted to threaded pipe placed at a greater depth in 1875, and improved its service further in 1876 when George Hill bought the company and enlarged some of the mains.[28]

In 1879 Alvaro Evans founded a competing water company and purchased the Reno Water Company and the Highland Ditch; the new company improved and enlarged the delivery system and excavated Highland Reservoir in 1879–80.[29] Although water became more accessible to residents during the 1870s and 1880s, its quality was notoriously poor. The ditch ferrying water from the reservoir was not covered, leading to contamination from corrals, feedlots, and animal carcasses. Furthermore, a strainer over the exit pipe from the reservoir had a tendency to come loose, allowing fish into the lines; as the lines reduced in size, the unhappy result in town was "Reno chowder."[30]

The water company reorganized again in 1889 as part of the Reno Water, Land, and Lights Company, combining previously existing water and gas companies. The new ownership had little effect on water quality—in 1895 the company officially advised residents to boil the water

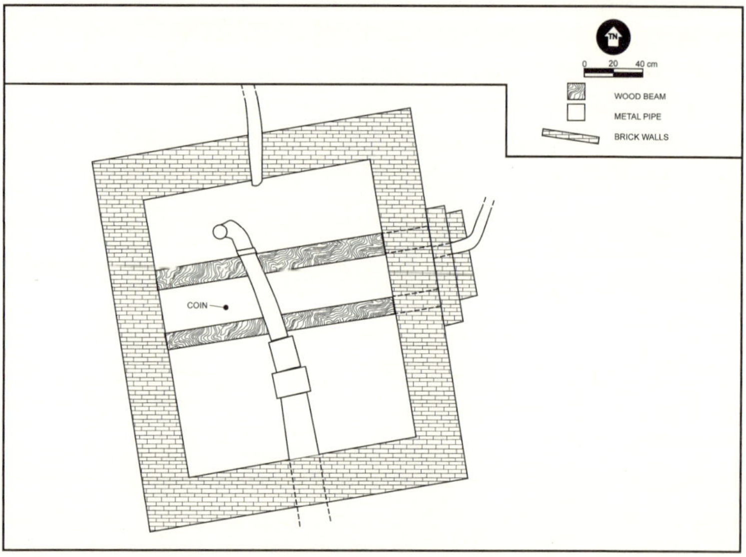


*Top:* Valve box and water line. Courtesy of WCRM, Inc.

*Bottom:* Brick utility access structure. Courtesy of WCRM, Inc.

before drinking it.[31] Citizens began pushing for the town to take over the company, but Reno was not yet an official municipality, and there were obstacles to overcome before this goal could be met. The results of the 1896 election called for town incorporation and municipal ownership of the Reno Water, Land, and Lights Company, but that was not the end of the matter. Owned by several wealthy and influential Reno residents, the powerful company fought the legislation and the newborn Reno town council for the next three years; it successfully retained self-ownership by pushing a disincorporation bill through the state legislature in 1899.[32] Governance of Reno reverted back to the county commission, against the wishes of the population.

Only when the need for a reliable source of drinking water reached near-crisis proportions did the community of Reno finally become an official town. For the first thirty-five years of its existence, Reno had no city government, partly because residents perceived such a body as being too controlling and expensive. Historian John Townley noted that "Washoe's electorate firmly believed its best government was the least government. Reno deferred town rule decade after decade, relying on a county commission to enact ordinances infrequently on demand."[33] This emphasis on individual freedom and general skepticism toward government control played into Reno's longtime identity as a permissive place where vices such as gambling were not only allowed but encouraged. In the case of the municipal water system, it was truly a bottom-up rather than top-down process that resulted in the establishment of a reliable water conveyance system—and, almost tangentially, of Reno's city government. The community ultimately incorporated in 1903, and the water system rapidly improved after its transfer to public ownership.

The water-related features discovered during the course of the ReTRAC project reflect different eras of infrastructure placement and upgrades. The oldest infrastructure feature found was a redwood valve box constructed with square machine-cut nails. The valve box contained a four-inch threaded iron water pipe and dated to 1875–1900. As mentioned earlier, threaded pipes were first adopted in 1875, and smaller-diameter pipes were phased out after improvements at the turn of the century. The use of square machine-cut nails in the construction suggests that the box was constructed closer to 1875 than to 1900, because this type of nail had been almost totally replaced by round-bodied wire nails, the same kind used today, by the latter date.

Another early urban infrastructure feature, a rectangular brick utility vault just west of Center Street, protected and provided access to three iron or steel water pipes ranging in diameter from two to six inches. An 1879 map shows a two-inch water line running east–west through this area, between the main line tracks and the Virginia & Truckee tracks and into the nearby Center Street cistern.[34] The two-inch pipe that ran across the bottom of the brick vault is probably this same line. The original construction date of the feature was likely between 1875 and 1905; its location directly above a threaded iron water line installed circa 1875 suggests it was built sometime after that year. A Dr. Henley's Wild Grape Root Bitters bottle found in the fill immediately outside the feature dates from 1866–1905. An 1896 quarter found near the floor of the structure probably indicates the approximate date of modification or filling in/abandonment.

We encountered portions of wood stave pipe dating to circa 1907 in two locations a few blocks west of the downtown core. This water conveyance feature reflects the spread of urban infrastructure outside the main business district during the early twentieth century. Workers most likely constructed the pipe as part of the water system established in

A partially collapsed segment of wood stave pipe. Courtesy of WCRM, Inc.

1907. The *Reno Evening Gazette* reported the near completion of the new city system, which would use Hunter Creek water:

> Now that the trench is completed there will be no more work done on the water system until the first car load of pipe arrives which will be some time within the next two weeks. . . . This pipe is made of wood and is twenty-two inches in diameter. It is bound together with steel bands and is the most modern wooden pipe manufactured. . . . As soon as this pipe arrives a score of men will be put to work laying and fitting it and it will then only be a few weeks until the clear pure mountain water is pouring into the water mains of Reno and into the hydrants of every home in the city.[35]

The pipe was made of curved, beveled redwood slats that fit together to form a cylinder; the slats were tightly wrapped with quarter-inch steel wire. This type of wooden stave pipe was commonly used for water and sewer lines between about 1890 and 1950, often with even larger diameters for industrial or heavy urban use.[36] The date the pipe was abandoned is unknown, but one source reports that pipes of this type had a life span of thirty-five years or more.[37]

## SEWER SYSTEMS

Reno's early sewage disposal system was similar to its water system in being late to develop and only sporadically successful until large-scale improvements were made by popular demand. Privies (outhouses) dug by private parties on their own property constituted the first waste disposal system; these quickly contaminated the groundwater and nearby wells. Soon after 1868, Reno's business owners constructed sewer lines that ran south from downtown businesses and hotels, through streets and alleys, and dumped directly into the Truckee River. The wastewater lines carried storm runoff and trash of every kind as well as raw sewage; many of the lines ended at street curbs, where shallow open ditches accumulated runoff, trash, and sewage. The debris was occasionally flushed away when water from one of the irrigation ditches was fed into the waste ditches. The river carried waste away during its high flow seasons, but the pileup of effluvia during the drier summer months was notoriously foul.

In 1887 county commissioners hired Colonel George Waring, a well-known engineer from San Francisco, to plan a new sewer system. He recommended combining all wastes into one high-flow outlet that would raise the river's level enough to carry all of it away. The county carried out Waring's plan, and local convicts installed more than 4 miles of pipe in 1887.[38] Residents slowly connected to the system, although some were loathe to abandon their privies. In 1889 the commissioners outlawed residential privies and required all residents to hook up to the city system. Even the earliest sewer pipes were at least six inches in diameter, the minimum recommended by Waring.[39] Improvements to the sewer system continued in the early twentieth century and included placement in 1910 of 21.174 miles of sewer pipe ranging in diameter from six to twenty-four inches.[40]

The only archaeological find associated with the historical sewer system was a brick manhole vault for accessing sewer lines, recorded just south of an intersection of two alleys south of Commercial Row between Lake Street and Evans Avenue. Ceramic pipes about twenty inches in diameter entered from the north and south at the bottom of the feature. This type of utility probably dates to the 1930s. The other municipal sewer- and storm drain–related features recorded during the course of the ReTRAC project were all large ceramic pipe segments of indeterminate date and association.

## GAS AND ELECTRICITY

Natural gas lighting and heating systems first became available to Reno residents in the late 1870s. The spread of city gas systems and the later transition to electrical power displayed a pattern of fitful stop-and-start improvements and standardizations much like those seen in the city's water and sewer systems. The community's businesses and residences first started using petroleum gas for lighting in 1876, when M. G. Elmore founded the Nevada Gas Works.[41] That autumn, a large crew of workmen began to lay pipe downtown, and construction began on the gas-generating plant. The first gas jet was lit on 16 November 1876.[42] By the mid-1880s citizens were lobbying to replace the smoky gaslights with electric ones, and construction on the Reno Electric Light Company's water-powered dynamo in the Truckee River commenced in 1886.[43] The electrical power generator was completed in 1887, and electric streetlights replaced most of the gaslights on Commercial Row and other downtown streets. By 1888 Reno had ninety-five electric streetlights.[44] The water-driven dynamo was somewhat unreliable because the river flow fluctuated, and in 1890 the company's new owners built a new steam-powered plant that improved the service. In 1889 county commissioners approved the Electric Light Company's request to place telegraph and power poles downtown. The new electrical poles and lines stood above the ground, creating what the *Nevada State Journal* called a "snarl of scaffolding and cables," until the city began placing electrical cables in underground conduits in the 1950s.[45]

Gas lighting was far from extinct, however; the gas company reorganized itself and extended its pipelines in 1889. The Central Pacific passenger depot built in that year was completely gaslit.[46] Gas was markedly cheaper than electricity for some time, and many consumers opted to keep using it for lighting until electricity became the dominant technology in the 1910s. Two gas lines discovered during the ReTRAC project date to the period between 1876 and 1915, when gas usage was most common in town. One was a redwood conduit containing small-diameter iron pipes insulated with tar; it ran east–west on the north side of the railroad tracks. The other gas line, in the same area, was identical but ran east–west on the south side of the tracks north of Commercial Row. Utility trenches dug later in the project at other points along the probable course of the gas line did not expose any more segments of the conduit, indicating that most of these early utility lines had been damaged or destroyed by improvements in the city's infrastructure system during the twentieth century.

Gas is, of course, a volatile material, and explosions from the ignition of gas leaks were fairly common in downtown Reno. Most of the explosions in the commercial district were small and caused only minor damage. One, however, was devastating—and was directly related to the older utility lines and long-forgotten ditches that ran below downtown buildings.

On 5 February 1957 a gas main under several large commercial buildings at the southeast corner of First and Sierra streets ruptured, resulting in three devastating explosions that leveled nearly an entire city block. Frank Spira and Adeline DuPratt were killed instantly; forty-nine others were injured, some critically.[47] One of the injured, Elizabeth Thompson, was comatose for more than six years before she died.[48] An investigation into the cause of the blast determined that the broken pipe traversed a segment of the Riverside Mill Ditch long buried under city streets and business blocks. The pipe had been installed over the ditch's concrete culvert and was not adequately supported by fill; as the soil around it settled, the pipe was placed under stress. When the stress combined with the extreme cold of that February, only a small jolt was required to break the pipe.[49] Once the leaking propane gas had mixed with enough oxygen, an explosion was inevitable. Investigators searching for more pockets of gas found more buried segments of the Riverside Mill Ditch, as well as part of the Sullivan-Kelly Ditch, that had long been covered over and forgotten.

## STREETS AND HIGHWAYS

Construction and maintenance of streets and connector routes was an important part of Reno's infrastructure development, and predictably became more significant after the automobile became the dominant form of transportation. Much has been written about "car culture" and its effects on cities and towns. The urban centers of the nineteenth-century West existed on a scale that a resident could navigate on foot, horseback, wagon, or carriage. Extensive railroad systems enabled quicker travel over longer distances. As cities grew, public transit systems became important elements of transportation. Streetcars were particularly common in western cities. The mass introduction of the automobile in the 1910s first meant merely that trolleys and horse-drawn wagons shared thoroughfares with cars. But as cars became more common, road construction began expanding to serve the needs of the car-owning public. Like the railroads before them, the location of automobile routes affected the development of nearby towns and cities.

Commercial Row was Reno's original thoroughfare; it paralleled the transcontinental railroad line through town, and most of the community's businesses were situated there. The business district grew with the city, soon expanding south down Virginia, Sierra, and Center streets. This pattern and direction of commercial growth continued until Lincoln Highway came through Reno. This interstate highway, established in 1913 but not completed until the 1920s, ran on Fourth Street several blocks north of the railroad tracks. Victory Highway/U.S. Highway 40 used the same route starting in 1925–26. U.S. 40 was one of the main routes across the United States, and in the 1950s it carried more automobile traffic than any other transcontinental road. Locals knew the thoroughfare as Truckee Highway and Verdi Highway, as well as Lincoln Highway and Victory Highway. Automobile traffic boomed in response to continued improvements in the route, and Reno benefited. The Fourth

Street corridor quickly became a second business district lined with elaborately designed auto courts, motels, restaurants, auto repair shops, and other businesses catering to a new kind of tourist: the road-tripper.

The city implemented a number of road improvements and realignments in the 1920s and 1930s to profit from the increasing interstate automobile traffic. One realignment was the Second Street underpass, constructed between 1928 and 1929, which provided an alternate business route for traffic moving through Reno on U.S. Highway 40 and was designed to improve automobile access to downtown.

In 1925 Reno business owners began to lobby for an extension of West Second Street to connect with the main highway and provide an alternate route that would bring more business to downtown. They argued that this extension would also eliminate a sharp turn and grade crossing at Vine Street where numerous accidents had occurred.[50] By 1928 the extension, which would include an underpass under the Southern Pacific main line tracks, had been approved by the city and negotiations were taking place with the railroad regarding costs and plans.[51] The project was ultimately funded jointly by the city, the county, and Southern Pacific.[52] Construction began on the underpass in October 1928,[53] and the city completed and dedicated the underpass and street extension in April 1929. Within five years city officials were considering altering or replacing it because the underpass was too narrow and the approaches from Fourth and Second streets were too abruptly angled.[54]

The ReTRAC work exposed a portion of the original underpass consisting of two parallel concrete walls located directly under the main railroad tracks, about twenty-seven meters (ninety feet) east of the second Second Street underpass. Between the walls, the fill under the railroad ballast was undifferentiated light brown to brown sandy clay. Outside the walls, the profile had well-defined stratigraphy, including a dark-stained soil layer over older railroad ballast. Both walls were only partially exposed, to approximately three meters (ten feet) down; for safety reasons they were not fully exposed to their bases.

Following the 1935 approval of a federal work-relief resolution allocating $200 million to grade-crossing improvement projects across the nation, Reno began seeking bids to build an entirely new underpass next to the existing one. This new underpass was designed to be wider and to pass diagonally under the Southern Pacific main line, diverging from Fourth Street immediately west of the present pass and eliminating the blind curve at each entrance.[55] It was completed in 1936. The city filled in and abandoned the old Second Street underpass after having used it for only seven years. The new underpass remained in use until 2004, when it was removed as part of the ReTRAC project.

In 1974 Nevada completed Interstate 80 through Reno. Typical of modern highway systems, the route bypassed Reno's major business districts, taking most traffic past both Fourth Street and downtown. The change hurt both of those commercial areas, and today many of Fourth Street's historic motels and auto courts are in sad disrepair. This pattern of development and abandonment based primarily on automobile traffic flow is reflected in many U.S. cities, and in the past few years has reached a new expression in the "big box" stores built on the outskirts of communities. Impractical to reach by foot and out of the way for many municipal bus systems, these businesses and their enormous parking lots are inextricably tied to cars.

Alarmed by the near abandonment of many historic business districts, many communities are embracing "Main Street" programs that aim to bring the focus back to the towns' physical and social hearts. Reno has not been as dramatically affected as some communities have by the changes in transportation networks during the twentieth century, but its Fourth Street corridor stands as a testament to a once-vibrant district now struggling to survive. Revitalization efforts continue, and the area has received attention for its spectacular architecture; many striking examples of "car culture" design do endure.

Like any other city, Reno continues to face infrastructure challenges as the population grows. Suburban sprawl has pushed the city limits much farther to the north, south, and west, requiring investment in more roads, a bigger water system, and a more powerful electrical grid. Natural processes continue to pose obstacles: the Truckee River floods occasionally, and the city lies in a seismically active area susceptible to earthquakes of magnitudes up to 7.0 on the Richter scale. The development of Reno's infrastructure is an ongoing process. It is not a glamorous part of city history, but it is typical of most urban centers; the archaeological examination of the ordinary things making up Reno's urban infrastructure helps to shift the focus to history on a smaller scale.

CHAPTER

5

# The Story in Broken Bottles

During the excavation of the railroad trench, Union Pacific rerouted train traffic to a "shoofly," or temporary parallel track, a short distance to the south. Because the shoofly had to be substantial enough to support the weight of enormous freight trains, it could not be just ties and rails on an unprepared ground surface; the route had to be prepared to engineered specifications. Mechanical scraping of the ground surface in an empty lot exposed several large charcoal stains and turned up an unexpected discovery: a pile of paper bottle labels marked FRANK BROS CO. RENO NV BOTTLERS. Research confirmed that this lot had once been the site of the Frank Brothers bottling operation.

The archaeological investigation of the Frank Brothers bottling plant revealed fifteen buried features, several of which could be directly linked to the bottling works. Most of the features were charcoal and ash stains and deposits representing the remnants of a lumber yard that occupied the parcel during the 1890s, before the Frank Brothers building was constructed; all of the lumber in this yard burned in a spectacular conflagration one night in 1900.[1] Other features were pieces of concrete foundations representing other buildings within the parcel. The site was a perfect example of an archaeological palimpsest—an area that experienced multiple occupations and uses over time, with each activity leaving its mark on top of, and sometimes dug into, those that came before it. As the Frank Brothers excavation proved, such sites can be complicated to decipher. The Frank Brothers site contained remnants of at least three different businesses representing occupations over a fifty-year period.

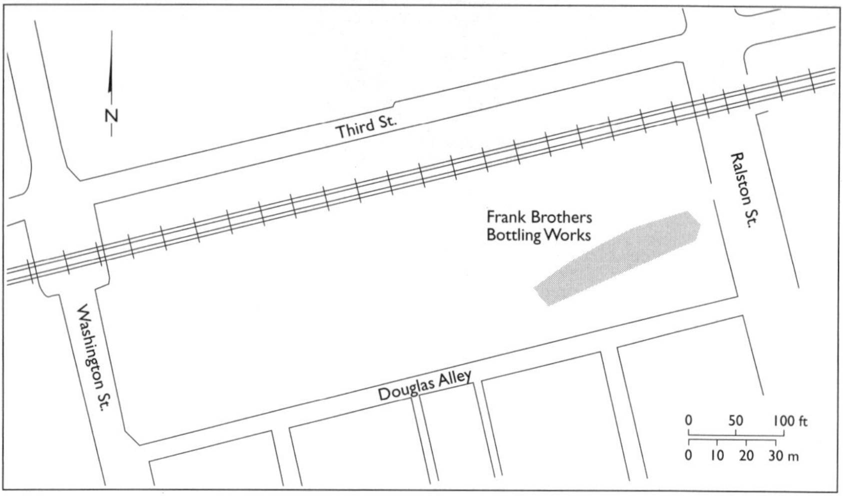


Location of the Frank Brothers site.

Frank Brothers bottle label. Courtesy of WCRM, Inc.

One feature was unmistakably linked to Frank Brothers: a pit full of tens of thousands of pieces of broken bottle glass. The artifacts found in this feature are discussed later in the chapter.

The archaeological remains of the Frank Brothers Bottling Works building represent a successful local business that operated for more than thirty years, between about 1903 and 1939. Frank Brothers was not a unique or even unusual commercial operation, nor was it the setting for a spectacular historical event. In fact, it was extremely typical of a successful family-owned enterprise that adapted to changing circumstances in order to survive. The site had little to say about human behavior as a whole, but when viewed in a larger historical context it revealed itself to be a rich source of knowledge. Thanks largely to information from local collaborators Ed Folsom and his daughter Darla Potter, researchers were able to explore what it would have been like to work at a bottling business during the 1920s and 1930s.

Historic period sites, especially in urban centers, are inevitably linked in some way to national or international patterns, or both. As product distribution patterns shifted and expanded during the late nineteenth century, due in large part to the connections created by railroads, goods once available only within a small geographical area gained a much larger customer base. A prospector visiting a small Nevada mining town for supplies could buy the same brands of lard, canned vegetables, or digestive medicine as a New York City banker or a London gentleman could. Patterns in distribution and consumption of these kinds of mass-produced goods are traceable through the artifacts found in archaeological sites, and differences can be examined on the local scale as compared to the larger national or international scale. Studies of these kinds of patterns are among the most common approaches in historical archaeology.

The Frank Brothers operation was a local business that provided both nationally and locally produced goods to its customers; that is, it existed within a large and multilayered context. An exploration of its day-to-day operations shows Frank Brothers to be representative of such local expressions of national economic and social patterns. Historical and archaeological examinations of Frank Brothers revealed information about the bottling industry, the development of commercial enterprise in western urban centers, and the way one business adapted to two twentieth-century events crucial in shaping the nation: Prohibition and the Great Depression.

Overview of the Frank Brothers site location.

## SODA BOTTLING AT THE TURN OF THE CENTURY

The processes and challenges of commercially bottling beverages have remained much the same throughout the history of the industry: producing or acquiring a product, enclosing it in an appropriate container, distributing the container to the market, reacquiring the container, washing it, and reusing it. Getting carbonated liquids to stay carbonated in a closed container without exploding was the first, and most fundamental, obstacle that beer and soda bottlers faced; solving this problem resulted in the development of different types of ceramic and, later, glass bottles. The constraints of transportation and distribution, as well as the needs of target markets, also influenced container styles. Bottles had to be durable enough to survive shipping and delivery but light enough to be moved efficiently. The different storage and service needs of outlets such as saloons, restaurants, grocery stores, retail liquor stores, and home trade required variations in bottle sizes and shapes, which in turn required different types of shipping crates. Changes in closure styles appropriate to specific bottle contents developed in response to many of the same pressures, in addition to such influences as consumer preferences and aesthetic trends. All of these changes were driven both by the economic market and by the social climate of the time, which encouraged technological change, and exemplify how social forces affect the development of technological systems.

Until the last third of the nineteenth century, the available manufacturing and shipping technologies limited the American bottling industry. Glass bottles were almost all individually mouth-blown, their finishes were nonstandardized, and they were largely shipped via freight wagons. Rapid advances in bottle-manufacturing techniques, innovations in bottle-filling and -closing techniques, and the establishment of reliable railroad connections between markets revolutionized the bottling industry. The development of the Owens semiautomatic and fully automatic bottle machines between 1892 and 1904 shifted bottle-manufacturing techniques away from hand-blown to mechanical methods that were much faster and cheaper.

Advances in bottling technology during the late nineteenth century largely involved the slow shift from hand- and foot-operated machines to power-operated machines. The 1892 patent of the crown cap closure was another important development for beer and soda bottlers. This new closure, the same kind seen on beer bottles today, was an improvement on internal closures such as the Hutchinson stopper and was argued to be a better method for closing bottles containing carbonated beverages. The new closure inspired changes in the design of bottle-syruping and -filling machines; the transition to the new designs happened slowly but steadily over the next few decades. Filler machines for the new closure were hand or foot operated until power-operated machines were introduced at the turn of the twentieth century. The power-operated crown filler system also fixed the cap to the finish, completing the filling and closing processes in quick automated steps and ensuring rapid adoption of the system.

Other improvements were concurrently taking place. New carbonation techniques included the use of liquid carbon dioxide and the introduction of several new types of carbonators that mixed the resultant gas with water.[2] Bottle washers also improved greatly during the early twentieth century, and power-operated soakers and washers became the industry standard. Advances in power-operated water filtration, an important first step for soda bottlers, led to quicker removal of suspended matter and enabled more efficient bottling.

Industrial-scale soda bottling began in the late nineteenth century but did not become commonplace until the early twentieth. The number of

American plants bottling soda nearly doubled between 1900 and 1910, and by 1920 there were more than 5,200.[3] The growth was largely due to the realization that home deliveries enabled bottlers to compete with soda fountains, and also increased consumers' demand for flavored carbonated beverages.[4] Some smaller bottlers began to bottle and deliver soda rather than distributing beer and liquor; others focused primarily on beer bottling and bottled soda only as a side project—their primary customers were saloons.

Small local bottlers tended to adopt new technologies more gradually than larger operations because of the expense of buying and installing new equipment and training workers to use it. To compensate, these smaller bottlers had to be creative in finding ways to adapt to the changing industry. Two developments in particular helped small bottlers in a competitive market: the use of automobiles rather than horses and wagons for deliveries, and investment in advertising and marketing. The brightly painted local delivery wagons of the late nineteenth century had conveniently served as both transportation and advertising. The adoption of delivery trucks led to changes in the way bottles were packed for delivery and to more widespread distribution. Historians John Paul and Paul Parmalee noted that "the growth of the industry essentially paralleled the development of a suitable vehicular conveyance and the increase in the potential number of customers available."[5] Most bottlers had incorporated truck transportation into their operations by 1915–20.

Railroad shipping had always been an important facet of late-nineteenth- and early-twentieth-century bottling distribution, and continued to be so even after the advent of the automobile. Until the development of interstate highway systems decades later, rail shipping would be the dominant mode of distribution for larger, national companies. High rail rates during the Great Depression did, however, lead to new approaches to transportation and distribution. Local franchising—described below—was one significant cost-cutting adaptation.

Marketing and advertising techniques changed along with national distribution patterns and the establishment of larger corporations during the early twentieth century. Improvements in printing technology sped production of newspapers and made printing of private advertising material more affordable. The bottling industry was quick to embrace advertising, as evidenced by *The Bottler's Helper,* a bottlers' guide published in 1907 that lists numerous useful advertising ideas as a necessary part of

Frank Brothers advertisement in the *Nevada State Journal*, 18 December 1911.

the business.[6] The increase in public exposure and improved delivery systems led to new outlets for distribution. The Prohibition era demand for soda pop may actually have been due as much to increased advertising as to the outlawing of alcohol.[7] Bottlers that had once distributed their wares primarily to saloons and restaurants had begun to deliver soda to corner groceries, neighborhood candy shops, and drugstore soda fountains between 1900 and 1920, even before national Prohibition.[8]

When the eighteenth amendment to the Constitution prohibited the production and sale of alcoholic beverages in 1920, the federal government effectively forced the nation to go "dry." American mainstream culture had been trending toward conservatism for some time. Deeply rooted political corruption on the local level had caused many Americans to call for overall reform. The country had recently been experiencing a heavy influx of immigrants—people drawn to America in hopes of finding a better life—and these newcomers were changing the landscape of U.S. cities. Rapid industrialization and the widespread abuse of workers by corporations had roused a burgeoning labor movement, some facets of which openly called for a socialist system. Prodded on in many cases by corporate-owned newspapers, and exacerbated by the looming specter of World War I, many Americans felt a growing fear—it seemed that everything was changing rapidly, not always for the better.

Progressive reform movements called for reform in education, government, and common vices in a bid to improve the overall integrity of the nation. Some Progressives included moral reform as part of their political and economic reform agenda and introduced legislation explicitly designed to "protect" citizens from drinking, prostitution, and gambling. The moral dimension of the Progressive movement may not have been topmost in the minds of many reformers, but members of the Women's Christian Temperance Union and similar temperance groups saw it as a crucial component of improving the nation. Many of the activist Progressive women's groups tied temperance to the crusade for women's right to vote.

When America entered World War I in 1917, reformers made a new argument for Prohibition: the grain used to make alcohol should instead be used as food for the Allied troops. Nevada responded to the wartime need by voting in November 1918 to ban the manufacture and sale of alcoholic beverages; the law went into effect on 17 December of that year.[9] Most of Reno's saloons and liquor stores went out of business or shifted toward the sale of other products as a result. Historian William Rowley noted that "without the war effort, the reform movement alone would not have been able to close the doors of Reno's saloons."[10]

Although Nevada adopted Prohibition early on, it quickly became clear that a dry state was a near impossibility. Law enforcement personnel could not keep up with the widespread manufacture and distribution of bootleg liquor. In January 1920 U.S. District Attorney William Woodburn summarized the problem in Reno: at least seventy-five bootlegging operations were active, whereas before Prohibition the town had only had about fifty saloons.[11] By early 1925 liquor law violators filled the jails of Washoe, Ormsby, and Churchill counties to capacity.[12] The *Carson City Daily Appeal* clearly stated the case against Prohibition in 1928:

Prohibition in Nevada has not been prohibition. It has kept the federal court busy for the past ten years, and today road houses, soft drink joints and home brew have taken the place of the licensed saloon. Despite the condemning of licensed saloons the fact must stick out to the drys that there was more law and order and less generally drinking under open saloon days than there is today. The sale of sugar, corn, corks, bottles, kegs and train loads of grapes is the best evidence of the assertion and the jails back up the history of the case.[13]

Reno resident Harold Curran, who graduated from the University of Nevada, Reno in 1930, recalled entering a speakeasy with some friends before basketball practice one day. Startled to see a policeman sitting at the bar, they hesitated in the doorway. But the bartender told them it was okay, so they entered and had a drink with the officer. Curran also recalled that the production of liquor for personal use was extremely common: "Anyone who could get enough money to do it was making liquor."[14]

Prohibition remained in effect until 1933, when the eighteenth amendment was finally repealed. The "noble experiment" was done in not just by Americans' desire to drink, but also by larger changes in the national mood, not to mention the immense costs of policing the thriving black market in alcohol. Up to 65 percent of the cases in federal district courts during Prohibition involved liquor law violators.[15]

National Prohibition had a significant effect on the American bottling industry between 1920 and 1933 because it totally eliminated the legal bottling and distribution of alcoholic beverages. To survive, local bottlers turned to the sale of soda pop, mineral water, and other nonalcoholic beverages. Some began bottling sauces, condiments, vegetable oil, or other products. Others continued to bottle alcoholic beverages for the black market, although this, of course, was not widely advertised. Since saloons were no longer a legal option, more and more businesses began distributing beverages through deliveries to homes and grocery stores. Part of the industry's coping strategy was to popularize larger bottles—quart size rather than six-ounce size—for home use.[16]

By the early 1930s and the beginning of the Great Depression, competition in the bottling industry was fierce. When shipping rates became so high that large national bottlers could not profitably ship their wares to distant points, the practice of franchising became common. Local bottlers would pay a larger producer for the right to use its trademark and methods, then produce and distribute the product on a local scale. Reno's Shoshone Bottling Company is an example; it was a small operation until the Coca-Cola Company awarded it a bottling franchise in 1930. The popularity of that brand kept the Shoshone operation afloat during the Depression and led to its later expansion.[17] By the late 1930s soft drink bottling across the country had become almost completely local in scale.[18]

Even bottlers like Frank Brothers, who had operated on a smaller scale to begin with, felt the effects of the Depression and the high price of rail shipping. Under this kind of economic pressure, other factors were felt more keenly as well. Unreturned bottles, for example, had always been a problem. Bottlers depended on the reuse of bottles, and it was essential for them to develop methods to keep track of their bottles and make sure customers held up their end of the bargain by returning them. *The Bottler's Helper* contains thirty pages of ideas from bottlers around the country on how to get customers to return their bottles in a timely and consistent manner, ranging from the printing and distribution of friendly reminders, to award raffles for conscientious bottle returners, to outright threats of litigation.[19]

Bottlers' need for a steady supply of bottles became particularly problematic during the Depression. Residential customers tended to keep bottles to use in their own pickling, preserving, brewing, and distilling. Home production of food and alcohol was a sensible and common coping strategy during lean times, and old beer bottles were perfect for homemade beer, wine, spirits, and ketchup.[20] The establishment of a dependable container deposit system, which became practically universal in 1933–35 and required all bottlers to collect a deposit on returnable containers, ensured a steady supply of bottles.[21]

During the Depression the two-cent deposit to be regained by returning used bottles was not something to be ignored.[22] Archaeologist Dave Valentine calculated that the 1930s bottle glass assemblage from a historical site near Las Vegas, Nevada, would have been worth $2.86 in deposits during the Depression.[23] That amount seems insignificant today, but Valentine's analysis provides a good illustration of just how much that would have meant to a worker in the 1930s. The average nonfarm income for the western United States in 1929 was $953 a year. Laborers at Hoover Dam earned $4 per day, a sum considered to be good pay; workers with specialized skills, such as concrete workers and electricians, were paid $6–12 a day. The $2.86 value of the bottle deposits would thus have represented a significant portion of a dam worker's daily wage. Valentine considered it "unlikely that this small fortune would just be abandoned, or allowed to accumulate during normal household beverage consumption," and hypothesized that the Las Vegas assemblage came from a bootlegging operation rather than a residential occupation.[24]

## THE FRANK BROTHERS BOTTLING WORKS

The story of the Frank Brothers site begins near the turn of the century, when a pair of Jewish brothers started a liquor distribution business in Reno. Ben and Sam Frank had operated a wholesale liquor business for seventeen years in San Francisco before they moved to Reno and opened their store at 228/230 North Virginia Street in 1903. Their bottling plant on Commercial Row appears to have been an outgrowth of this earlier wholesale liquor operation. Frank Brothers' newspaper advertisements during the first few years of business in Reno noted that the store carried various wines, champagnes, liquors, mineral water, and bar supplies.[25] The company incorporated in 1904 as a wholesale and retail liquor dealer, with shareholders Leon Frank, Sam Frank, and Ben Frank. Ben Frank managed the business. If the company was doing any of its own bottling or had a storage warehouse separate from its store on Virginia

Sam Frank, Myron Frank, and Ben Frank in front of their Virginia Street store, ca. 1910. Courtesy of the Nevada Historical Society.

Street at that time, it may not have been at the Commercial Row location. Research turned up no historical references to such enterprises.

The *Nevada State Journal* for 18 April 1905 notes improvements to the Frank Brothers storefront on Virginia Street that "will result in more than doubling the present capacity of their store."[26] The improvements appear to have mostly involved enlarging storage areas, which again suggests that this was the only building used by Frank Brothers at that time. The store at 228/230 North Virginia Street remained the main office and public contact point for the company until sometime between 1917 and 1920, when city business directories indicate that the office moved to 217 North Virginia Street.[27] The new office seems not to have included a store or storage area. By that time, most of the business was likely being conducted directly from the bottling works/warehouse west of downtown. The state of the Frank Brothers business in the 1920s is largely unknown, although it appears that the brothers had shifted away from wholesaling and toward direct distribution.

In the early 1930s Frank Brothers was a small-scale operation run more or less by one employee, Pierre "Pete" Tachoire, assisted by Ben Frank's young grandson Ed Folsom. Folsom had his first job at Frank Brothers at age thirteen or fourteen, working part time for his grandfather there in 1930–32. He was our primary source of information regarding day-to-day operations at the plant. Folsom recalled helping to mix syrup, move bottles to washing stations, label bottles, box the finished product, clean the shop, and assist Tachoire with deliveries. The company's customers included bars, wholesale stores, and a brothel on First Street. Ben Frank's son Myron (Ed Folsom's stepfather) had also worked there as a youth, and lost the little finger from his right hand when it was crushed between beer barrels.

The exact construction date for the bottling plant is unclear, but the building was standing by the beginning of 1910, when the business had at least seven employees; the plant was slightly damaged by a small roof fire that January.[28] Located on West Commercial Row between Ralston and Washington streets, the building was constructed of wood, had electric power, and included cold storage areas. The ability to store syrups, extracts, and even water in refrigerated areas meant longer-lived ingredients and a higher-quality product. Availability of electric power meant that the facility was able to use power-operated machinery rather than hand- and foot-operated equipment. The business may have used foot-operated machinery for some time, though. The Shoshone Coca-Cola Bottling Company started out in 1924 using a foot-operated pedal filler and washing bottles by hand,[29] so clearly, small bottlers could successfully operate in Reno at that time without the latest technological innovations.

The Frank Brothers bottling plant was located five blocks west of the downtown intersection of Virginia Street and Commercial Row, and was probably chosen because of its proximity to the industrial activities historically present in that part of town. The plant was accessed by a railroad spur line that ran northwest–southeast through the parcel and enabled easy offloading of materials onto the building's loading platform. This part of town was home to at least two other earlier bottling operations: the Buffalo Beer Depot and the Wieland Bottling Works. All situated within one square block, the plants constituted a small bottling district within the mixed industrial/residential neighborhood.

A 1910 *Nevada State Journal* article refers to the Frank Brothers building as the "Budweiser bottling depot" as well as "the warehouse and bottling depot of the Frank Brothers Co.," confirming the 1918 Sanborn fire insurance map's label of "Anheuser-Busch Beer Bottling."[30] The Frank Brothers Company was a local distributor of Anheuser-Busch beer, and bottled Budweiser and Blue Label brands shipped to the plant for distribution to businesses and family trade. The plant also bottled and distributed several brands of mineral waters, wines, and liquors.

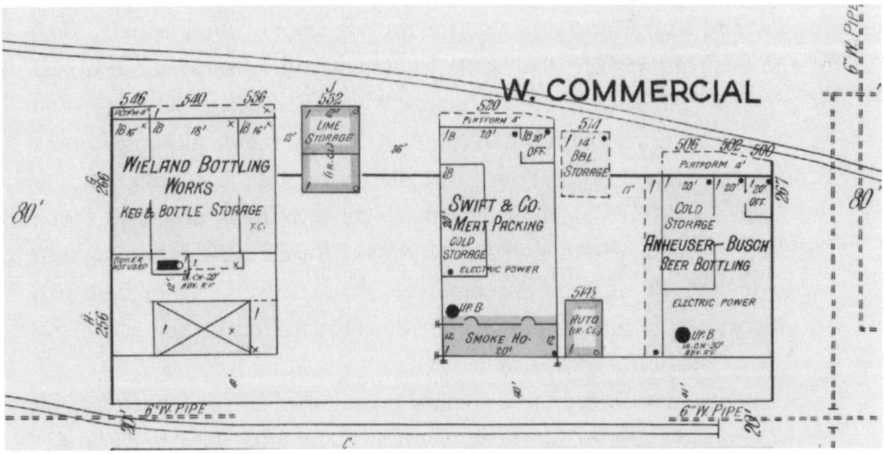


The Frank Brothers building (labeled "Anheuser-Busch Beer Bottling") and Wieland Bottling Works as shown on the 1918 Sanborn fire insurance map. Courtesy of Special Collections, University of Nevada, Reno, Library, and the Mary B. Ansari Map Library.

Frank Brothers delivery wagons in front of the Virginia Street store, ca. 1906. The man driving the wagon to the right may be Pete Tachoire. Courtesy of the Nevada Historical Society.

Like other small bottling operations, Frank Brothers actively advertised in local newspapers. Advertisements appeared in the *Nevada State Journal* and *Reno Evening Gazette* for the life span of the business. Most of the ads emphasized the better-known brands that Frank Brothers distributed—Budweiser, Cresta Blanca Wines, Old Tyler Whiskey—and many noted the company's dedication to family trade. Although Frank Brothers was largely a local operation delivering soda, beer, and liquor to the Reno-Sparks area, a 1904 newspaper advertisement describes Frank Brothers as the distributors of Bartlett Water for the state of Nevada.[31] In the early days, Frank Brothers employees made deliveries from the North Virginia store via horse and wagon; later they used a truck to make deliveries from the bottling works.

Frank Brothers responded to state Prohibition in 1918 and national Prohibition in 1920 in the same way that many other beer bottlers did: the company turned to the bottling and distribution of soda pop to survive. Folsom remembered preparing soda by mixing sugar and water by hand with a wooden paddle—this hand-mixing of sugar, flavoring, and water into an overhead crock was typical of turn-of-the-century techniques.[32] Employees used a gravity feed to transfer flavored syrup from a machine to the sugar water solution, added carbon dioxide, and bottled the result.

Folsom recalled soda flavors including grape punch, Orange Crush, sarsaparilla, and Coca-Cola; labels for strawberry- and lemon-flavored sodas were also found during excavation of the site. The strawberry, lemon, and sarsaparilla labels found during archaeological investigations show that Frank Brothers' products were similar to those from other soda bottling operations of that size during that period. Historian John Riley noted that "the smaller bottling plants usually limited their flavors to the few included in a common trade classification which, during the closing decades of the 1800's, came to be known as the 'red, white, black, and brown' line of sodas. This had particular reference to strawberry, lemon, sarsaparilla, and cream soda (vanilla)."[33] Grape punch and "cloudy orange" soda like Orange Crush were among the flavors that became available around 1915, and Coca-Cola was in wide distribution by the time the Frank Brothers plant opened.[34] Only much larger operations bottled more than a few flavors of soda.

During the 1930s Frank Brothers was also the local distributor for Bee brand playing cards. This may have been a response both to the Depression-era drop in business and to the relegalization of all forms of gambling.

Folsom's information indicates that the Frank Brothers bottling plant contained the standard equipment of an early-twentieth-century operation: a bottle washer, a machine for syruping and filling bottles, and a carbonator, as well as two cold storage areas cooled by a refrigerator plant, an office, and other miscellaneous storage. The building had four entrances. Two were small doors, one opening into the office at the building's northeast corner, the other opening into the south end of the building from Douglas Alley. The other two entrances were for loading and unloading goods; one was a sliding door in the building's north end opening onto a loading platform adjacent to the spur line, and the other was in the east side of the building, facing Ralston Street and opening onto a delivery truck loading platform. The building had a crawl space, but not a full basement. Folsom recalled that bottles broken during shipping or the bottling process were thrown into a large garbage container, but he could not pinpoint its location.

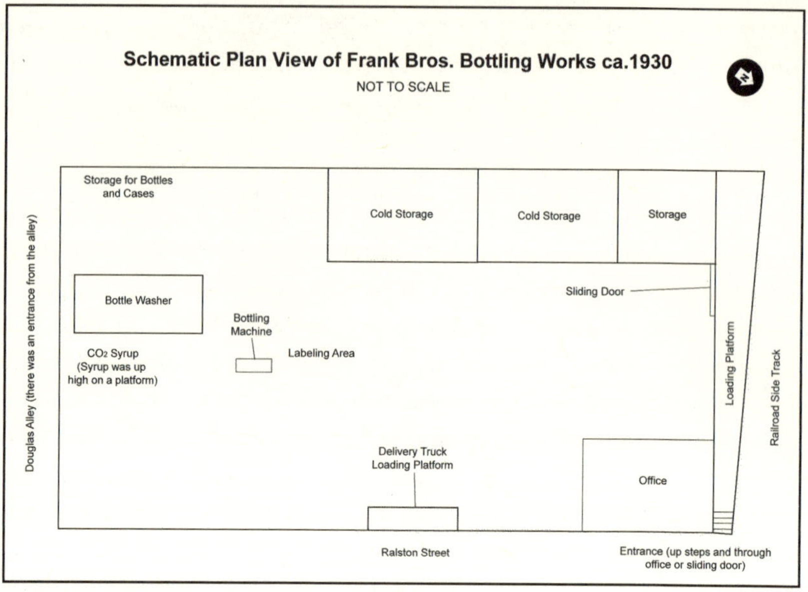


Layout of the bottling works, ca. 1930. Drawing by Darla Potter using Ed Folsom's recollections, 2003.

Frank Brothers went out of business in 1939, another victim of the Depression, and Home Lumber Company took over its plant for use as a warehouse. The building was abandoned and demolished in 1964, and the whole parcel was left empty and used as a parking lot. We do not know all of the reasons why Frank Brothers went out of business, but they were likely related to the company's small, local nature. A history of soft drink bottling written by John Paul and Paul Parmalee details a number of reasons why small bottlers of Illinois failed. These include an unfavorable location; slow or nonexistent growth in the bottler's city; inability to install new, modern equipment; failure to offer a diversified array of sodas; and insufficient advertising.[35] All of these factors are likely to have affected Frank Brothers to some extent.

Luckily, Ben and Sam Frank had other ongoing business ventures. They had established the Grand Central Garage on the corner of South Virginia and Liberty streets in 1925, and Ben focused his efforts there.[36] The Grand Central Garage was one of Reno's largest and best-known businesses, and included a service station as well as a large parking garage; it remained in operation until 1966. Ben Frank's son Myron took over management duties from his father in 1937. Sam Frank managed cattle ranches in Churchill and Lander counties and was a longtime member of the Reno City Council. He was appointed acting mayor of Reno in 1933 on the death of the officeholder, and unsuccessfully ran for the office in 1935. Both brothers were married and raised families, and some of their descendants live in Reno today.

## ARCHAEOLOGICAL FINDINGS

Archaeological investigations of the Frank Brothers site exposed fifteen buried features, including a pit of broken glass that proved to be a rich source of information. The artifact assemblage from the pit consisted predominantly of broken bottle glass that had been dumped into a shallow depression west of the building. This depression may have been a natural low spot but was more likely an excavated pit. The feature contained two deposits: the primary refuse deposit, an extremely high concentration of bottle glass mixed with small amounts of other debris; and a secondary deposit that contained dark charcoal-stained sediment with a much lower artifact density. The feature's exposed extent covered an area measuring approximately sixteen feet east–west by fifteen feet north–south. It also extended an unknown distance to the south, beyond the shoofly right-of-way onto inaccessible private property.

We excavated a sample of the primary glass deposit, approximately four meters (thirteen feet) square by half a meter (one and a half feet) deep, and collected 44,767 bottle glass fragments from it. Of these, 75 intact or nearly intact bottles and 652 smaller fragments contained diagnostic information such as dates of manufacture, types of bottles, and maker's marks. All of the specific manufacturing dates that could be determined fell between 1926 and 1939, confirming that the deposit was associated with known dates of Frank Brothers operation. The most commonly represented date of manufacture was 1928. The diagnostic glass assemblage overwhelmingly dated to the later Prohibition- and Depression-era operations of the bottling plant, not to its earlier years as a bottler and distributor of beer, liquor, and mineral water. It is likely, in fact, that the glass dump represents just the last few years of the bottling operation.

It must be remembered that the 1926–39 date range represents dates of bottle manufacture, not necessarily of discard. As archaeologist William Adams has shown in assessments of nonindustrial bottle glass assemblages, there is a time lag, often years long, between the time an artifact is manufactured and the time it finally enters the archaeological record.[37] The time lag for an industrial bottler's assemblage is not known.

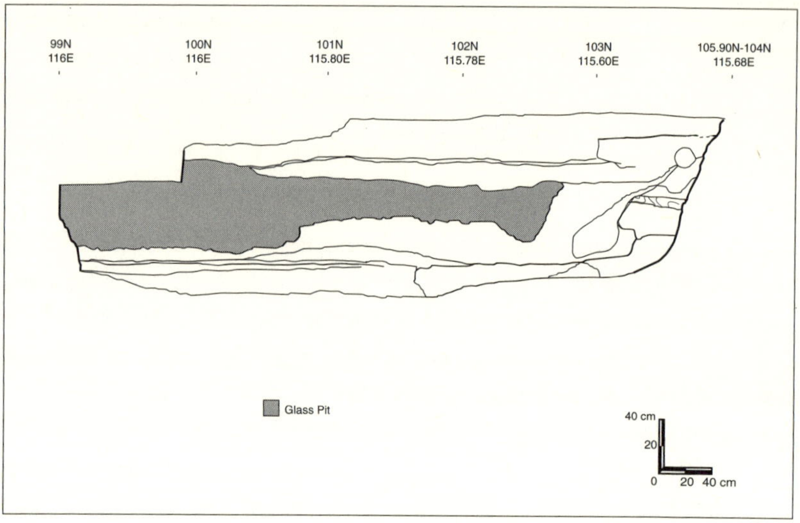


Profile view of a portion of the glass-filled pit. Courtesy of WCRM, Inc.

Other diagnostic items recovered from the glass dump encompassed a variety of materials, including several thousand Frank Brothers paper labels ranging from wholly intact labels to fragments. A partial body of an aqua bottle still had the remnants of one of these labels adhering to it. The feature also contained many artifacts representing remnants of the bottle-filling process, including ninety-four glass filler tube fragments and twenty-seven of the conical "nibs" that held the tube in position and compressed a washer against the top of the bottle to form a seal. Several of the nibs still had portions of the glass tubing in place. Bottles were filled by either raising the bottle to a filling head or lowering the head onto the bottle. In either instance, filling was through a glass tube that extended nearly to the bottom of the bottle, allowing it to fill from the bottom up.

Also recovered were 407 fragments of crown bottle caps, some with the composition cork liners that date from 1909 to about 1955, and some with the aluminum dot developed when it was determined that the cork imparted a flavor to beer, dating to 1916. Small fragments of equipment associated with an automated carbonator and an automated syruper-filler were also present, confirming the presence of these technologies at one time.

The glass dump was notable for the many different bottle types and sizes represented, but the most dominant types were those that would be expected in a beverage-bottling company. Most of the intact bottles were cylindrical, closed with a crown cap finish (the most common type for beverages), and were made by an automatic bottle-making machine. The presence of bottles of other sizes and closure styles confirms that the company was an active participant in the bottle returning and refilling practice that was common nationwide during the early twentieth century.

Ed Folsom recalled the company washing and refilling bottles brought in by customers, and remembered new bottles arriving from a California Bay Area bottle maker via train on the spur line in the parcel.[38] The artifact assemblage suggests that Frank Brothers may have followed the common practice of reusing just about any bottle brought in. While it was illegal for a bottler to reuse bottles embossed with the logo of another bottler, it appears to have been Frank Brothers' policy to allow consumers to bring in their own bottles to be refilled with a beverage of their choice. Whether customers waited while the bottles were cleaned and refilled, and whether Frank Brothers charged a deposit on such bottles is unclear. The variety of marks, of both product and bottle manufacturers, recovered from the glass dump suggests it was the company's policy to accept any refillable bottle, at least in its last few years of operation.

The types of marks found on bottles and fragments recovered from the feature support Folsom's recollection of new bottles coming from California; the single most common mark was that of the Illinois Pacific Glass Company, a major San Francisco glass manufacturer. The next most common mark was that of the Pacific Coast Glass Works and its successor, the Pacific Coast Glass Company. Both Pacific Coast and Illinois Pacific became holdings of the Owens Illinois Glass Company in 1932, when the combined firm began to use the general Owens Illinois makers mark.

Two artifact types in particular support the contention that Frank Brothers may have had a policy of filling any bottles that came its way, or at least did not actively refuse to do so: nonlocal bottles bearing the marks of nonfranchised brands such as the Red River Lumber Company, and fragments embossed with the Pluto Water mark. Pluto Water was a popular mild laxative beverage that was neither franchised nor locally bottled. Bottles like this would not have been part of a standard shipment straight from a glass manufacturer to the bottling plant, but would have passed through other hands on their way to reuse by Frank Brothers.

The most intriguing piece of evidence for indiscriminate bottle refill-

Broken bottle finish with nib. Courtesy of WCRM, Inc.

ing was the presence of internal closure-type bottles displaying a distinctive pattern of breakage at the lip or finish. These types of bottles could not be closed with crown bottle caps and may be evidence of the company using the crown filler machine to refill non-crown cap bottles. The crown filler machine was standard by the 1910s–20s, as described above, and was not designed for use with non-crown cap closures. An unusual artifact illustrates the point: a broken, non-crown cap bottle finish found with a complete nib and its attached glass tubing fragment and washer wedged into it—here is a bottle that probably stalled the filling line. In short, the archaeological evidence suggests that one of the company's responses to the financial strain of the 1920s and 1930s was to concentrate on family trade to the extent that it would refill any bottle returned to the plant for reuse.

Taken together, the historical accounts and archaeological remains of the Frank Brothers Bottling Works highlight one local business's adaptations to the pressures of larger social and economic forces. Like other small bottlers of the early twentieth century, Frank Brothers changed its marketing and distribution patterns as the market demanded; it shifted from wagon to truck delivery of its products, advertised in local newspapers, and delivered to multiple types of outlets. Because it was a distributor for large national products, one would expect Frank Brothers to have had up-to-date equipment that enabled efficient production and distribution of beverages. However, the recollections of teenage employee Ed Folsom show that at least in the early 1930s, Frank Brothers was a small operation that may have lagged behind in some aspects of technology adoption.

The company responded actively to the economic strain brought on by national Prohibition by switching over to bottling and distributing soda pop, and probably by increasing its distribution to residences and small retail outlets such as grocery stores. While Frank Brothers actively participated in the standard bottle return-refill-reuse model typical of early-twentieth-century bottlers, it seems to have taken this practice to an extreme by attempting to refill practically any type of bottle returned to its plant, even those without a crown cap closure. This was a direct response to the economic demands of the Great Depression and a distinctively local adaptation to larger patterns of distribution. Frank Brothers was directly linked to national systems of distribution, and it responded to and reinterpreted larger economic patterns on a local scale. The overwhelming evidence for common reuse of bottles is intriguing because it represents one company's attempt to cope with the economic pressures imposed by the Great Depression and Prohibition on small local businesses.

# CHAPTER 6

# African American-Owned Businesses in the Lake-Evans Block

About seven blocks east of the Frank Brothers parcel, preparation of the shoofly grade exposed another site. The removal of asphalt from a parking lot between Lake Street and Evans Avenue, south of the railroad tracks, uncovered multiple features: several brick rubble concentrations, a mottled charcoal and ash stain, and part of a brick wall. Archival research revealed that this area of the Lake-Evans block had contained three adjoining brick buildings dating to the turn of the century. The buildings housed many different businesses, both industrial and recreational, over the years. Their longest-lived and best-known occupants were the Harlem Club and the Dixie Club, both black-owned clubs representing part of a small twentieth-century African American commercial district at the edge of Reno's historically segregated downtown.

The initial archaeological testing, and later more extensive excavation, of the Lake-Evans block showed that most of its subsurface features were fragmentary building foundation remnants. With the exception of two features, they were too damaged and deteriorated from previous demolitions to provide much information about their construction or use. These two features—the Harlem Club building's basement and the foundation wall of the Dixie Club building immediately adjacent—were in good condition. The basement's walls, constructed of native rounded cobbles mortared together, exhibited characteristics typical of turn-of-the-century basement and foundation construction. Thanks to local collaborator Lonnie Feemster, researchers established contact with Wayne Crawford, a Reno resident who lived in the basement for several years when he was a child. Crawford's stepfather, Armster Embry, was a later owner of the building, and he and his family lived in a basement apartment there. Crawford was able to provide crucial details about the building and the operation of the club during its later years.

It is easy to think of archaeology as being all about artifacts, but much can be learned from landscapes and from features that are found in context. The Harlem Club building's basement is a perfect example. The research team was of course disappointed, though not surprised, to find that the basement's contents were not perfectly preserved in place, but the nature of the basement structure itself proved interesting.

An unstratified mix of historical and modern artifacts was present both inside and outside the building vestiges, but no trash dumps or other intact deposits were found. The mixed artifact assemblage reflected the parcel's long period of use and known modern disturbances, as did the fragmentary building vestiges. Much of the fill in the basement dated to the time of the demolition of the parcel's last building in the late 1970s, and represented a single event: after the brick building was knocked down and removed, its intact basement was filled with dirt and the whole block was paved over. While some of the fill dirt may have come from another location, a number of artifacts within it were clearly associated with the twentieth-century club—fragments of jukebox records, matchbooks, an earring, a keno ball, and even a die with HARLEM CLUB on it. The presence

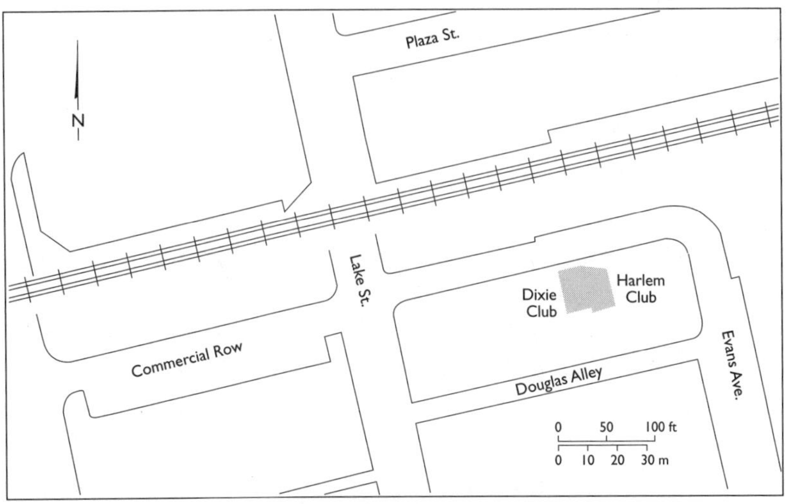


Location of the Lake-Evans block.

Harlem Club die, Keno ball, and earring. Courtesy of WCRM, Inc.

of these scattered artifacts evokes memories of a place that existed largely as a result of the institutionalized racism of Reno's recent past.

Reno's African American population has never been large, but it has been an important presence in the city from the beginning. In 1870, two years after Reno was established, the federal census counted 324 blacks in Nevada; of that number, 36 lived in Washoe County, with 22 of them residing in Reno proper.[1] Virginia City had the highest number of African American residents, with 90; at that time the Comstock was the most densely populated part of Nevada, full of people of all ethnicities who came in pursuit of mining riches. Nevada's black population stayed under 1,000—varying from a low of 134 in 1900 to a high of 664 in 1940—until the post–World War II period.[2] The 1950 census recorded a jump in the population to 4,302, representing an African American influx related to increased employment opportunities at military bases and elsewhere during the postwar boom.[3]

Reno, and indeed all of Nevada, was no different from most other places when it came to discrimination against minority groups, most visibly African Americans, Native Americans, and Asian Americans; racism was commonplace and blatant. A November 1904 article in the *Nevada State Journal* reports on the Reno Police Department's open policy of arresting and expelling all unemployed blacks: "Chief Leeper has decided to drive every vagrant negro from the city and those who do not obey the comands [*sic*] of his officers are immediately arrested and placed in the cells. This may be a little different from the regular proceedings of the law, but it is working good in Reno and the town will soon be cleared of the black element."[4] Another *Journal* article about a 1924 Prohibition raid on a black club shows that little had changed over the past twenty years. Eight men were arrested on suspicion of buying drugs and liquor. Although none of the alleged contraband was found and they were not charged with a crime, the newspaper stated they "probably will be given 24 hours in which to leave the city."[5]

By the 1950s local African Americans applied the label "Mississippi of the West" to Nevada as a whole and Las Vegas, Hawthorne, and Reno in particular—not because of violence or discriminatory laws on the same scale as notoriously racist Mississippi, but because of the damaging pervasive racism. Historian and civil rights activist Elmer Rusco noted that while Nevada was not as bad as Mississippi, it "was worse than most states, certainly worse than California in many respects."[6] Until 1959 it was illegal for blacks and whites to marry. Many employers excluded African Americans from all but the lowest-level jobs, and developers wrote deed covenants excluding blacks and Native Americans from buying houses in most neighborhoods. Most visibly, the majority of businesses downtown denied them service. Onie Cooper recalled, "We couldn't go in anywhere . . . it was disgusting. It made me feel very, very small and very, very upset."[7]

Until the passage of the Civil Rights Act of 1964, African Americans in most parts of the United States were regularly denied housing, job opportunities, and access to commercial businesses, and had no legal recourse. Racial discrimination in Reno severely limited housing, employment, and recreational options for African American residents. Dolores Feemster remembered being "maybe the only black working downtown. I caught heck from everybody."[8] Norma Washington stated, "I would have been 'too black' to do anything but clean hotel rooms or clean out spit cups. The men could only be janitors or porters. There were no opportunities for us."[9]

Most downtown casino and hotel owners did not allow African Americans to patronize their establishments, and the general social climate was hostile to them. Discrimination was not limited to the downtown commercial district—racist attitudes also limited access to home ownership. Most of Reno's African American residents lived in one of two places: a small neighborhood in the northeastern part of town or Black Springs, a cluster of homes just north of town on Highway 395.

In a 1971 interview, Reno resident Howard Gloyd pointed out that racial violence can cover a wider range of discriminatory activities than just bodily harm, and that Nevada had seen its share:

> There has been racial violence in Nevada in terms of unfair employment practices, racial violence in terms of the state of Nevada enacting an inadequate civil rights bill, in terms of the state of Nevada developing a non-functional Equal Rights Commission, things like that, that's violence. Things like public accommodations, you know, people like Charlie Mapes down there, violence; lack of equal opportunities, which creates sometimes hungry children in the state because their pop can't get a job because he's Black, that's violence. The lack of equal rights on a man's ability to do—we've got a lot of pretty sharp Black people in this state that are not doing anything, can't really earn money. You got Black people with all kinds of degrees working in bars and working as whatever they can find to do in this state, who want to stay in this state. . . . These are very violent things.[10]

Historian Guy Rocha credited the label "Mississippi of the West" as an effective way to "shame the Silver State and compel its lawmakers and others to address the problem of institutional racism. . . . [It] was a provocative rhetorical measure to elicit positive change in race relations, and it worked."[11] Led by the Reno-Sparks NAACP branch and partnered with branches in Las Vegas and Hawthorne, Nevada's black population fought for years to end public and private racial discrimination. As the casinos were the highest-profile discriminators in town, not to mention the biggest employers, Reno's civil rights activists directed most of their protests at them. Discrimination in housing continued well into the 1970s, when Governor Mike O'Callaghan successfully pushed a statewide open housing law through the legislature.[12] Less overt racial discrimination nevertheless continues today.

African American entrepreneurs in Reno, as in other cities, had long provided services for their own community. These services included bars and clubs, which have historically been important social gathering places for ethnic groups as well as repositories of common experience and memories. The Harlem Club and the Dixie Club, along with other black-owned businesses in Reno, represented active local adaptations to an environment in which options were limited. Both businesses provided recreational opportunities to patrons who were barred from entering white-owned casinos, restaurants, and hotels downtown. The Dixie Club operated for at least seventeen years, from about 1932 to 1949, and the

Harlem Club, later renamed the Soul Club, operated at this location for twenty-nine years, from 1948 to 1977. The businesses of the Lake-Evans block proved to be economically effective, as well as socially necessary, responses to a climate of prejudice.

Studies of African American–related sites of the twentieth century must consider the social force of racial discrimination. Archaeologists Paul A. Shackel, Eric L. Larsen, and others have argued that racial segregation creates a "landscape of conflict" that is visible physically as well as socially.[13] Meanings associated with these landscapes change over time, and as Shackel noted, "understanding how and why some groups tend to remember a particular past, while others forget or ignore a past, is an important issue for critically evaluating and knowing how people understand landscapes."[14] Social forces such as segregation have physical as well as social and cultural manifestations, and marginalized groups' responses to social forces sometimes include the conscious manipulation of physical objects and spaces in order to reinforce or reinterpret cultural identities. This is where archaeology, written history, and memory come together.

The history of Reno's African American clubs is rooted in the earliest years of the Lake-Evans block. This was one of the first business districts to develop in Reno, containing prominent commercial operations as early as the 1870s. The block's location directly south of the Virginia & Truckee Railway tracks shaped its physical growth, as the tracks ran down East Commercial Row in front of the block and then curved south down Peavine Street (now Evans Avenue), cutting off the parcel's northeast corner.

The businesses of the Lake-Evans block developed in three distinct episodes. The first episode, between about 1870 and 1899, began with the establishment of the long-lived Pyramid House saloon and lodgings and was marked by a slow and steady increase in commercial development. Although the block included one small industrial building—an oil warehouse—it was dominated by entertainment- and service-related businesses including hotels, saloons, restaurants, brothels, and a bowling alley. Its several small dwellings appear to have been related to the nearby commercial businesses. The block's proximity to downtown ensured steady growth, while its physical and psychologically perceived distance from Reno's peak-value intersections planted the seeds for its later development into notoriety as "that part of town." Close to China-

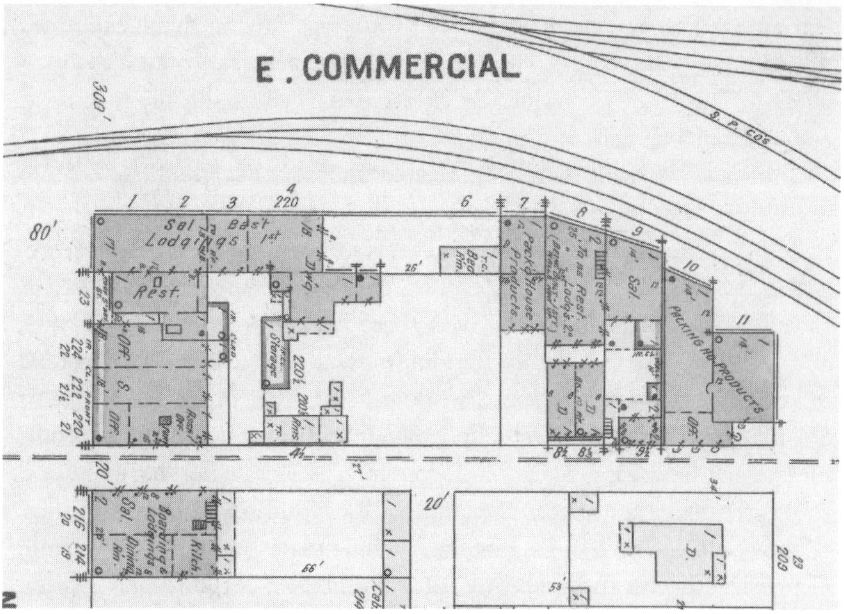


The Lake-Evans block as shown on the 1904 Sanborn fire insurance map. Courtesy of the Nevada Historical Society and the Mary B. Ansari Map Library.

town and the red-light district, the block was just north of the den of vice and iniquity known as the Tenderloin.

The second episode of development occurred between 1899 and 1904, and was marked by a distinct burst of activity resulting in the construction of multiple large brick buildings along East Commercial Row and Lake Street. This episode was part of the general economic growth that marked Reno's development during the first twenty years of the twentieth century. Industrial occupants increased to include several warehouses, slightly changing the nature of the block. Overall, though, recreation-related businesses such as saloons, restaurants, and hotels continued to dominate the location. Among the structures built during this period were three new brick buildings with angled fronts facing onto Commercial Row. Their placement and angled construction were clear accommodations to the Virginia & Truckee tracks, and their shapes maximized the amount of useful interior space. These buildings stood into the late twentieth century and eventually housed the Dixie Club and the Harlem Club. Several small dwellings were also present, but their relationship, if any, to the block's commercial businesses is unknown.

This pattern continued on through the 1910s and into the early 1920s:

businesses were consistently saloons, restaurants, and lodgings, with a few industrial and service occupants appearing periodically. This time period also marked the last significant physical development of the block until the demolition of most of the parcel's eastern brick buildings and construction of the New China Club in the 1950s. After 1904, the buildings appear to have maintained the same basic configurations aside from a few small additions and exterior/interior cosmetic renovations.

The third episode of development, from roughly 1920 to the 1970s, was notable not for its physical evolution but for the social and cultural environment in which it took place. In response to Prohibition, speakeasies began to occupy the brick buildings in the Lake-Evans block. African Americans were the primary owners of these clubs from as early as 1932, and they provided a service not only to the underserved local and visiting African American populations but apparently to all customers in search of alcohol.

At least as early as the 1930s and extending through the late 1970s, the area bounded by Commercial Row, Douglas Alley, Lake Street, and Peavine Street (Evans Avenue) became known as a predominantly African American commercial area. South of Douglas Alley, much of the rest of the city block housed Italian American-owned businesses—grocery stores and hotels such as the Toscano Hotel and the Columbo Hotel, all part of another small ethnic commercial district known as Little Italy. As noted in chapter 1, Reno had at least one other Little Italy, an architecturally distinctive neighborhood on the west side of town that was residential rather than commercial in nature. The best-known building in the southern part of the Lake-Evans block was the Pincolini—later Mizpah—Hotel, which became the anchor of Little Italy when it was completed in 1930. A 2006 fire killed twelve residents of the Mizpah Hotel and damaged part of the building; the city of Reno demolished the historic landmark in 2007.

Several Chinese American-owned businesses were also present in the block, hearkening back to the long history of Reno's Chinatown in that general area. Businesses run by Basques, French, and African Americans likewise show that the area was not exclusively Italian. Local historian Albin J. Cofone pointed out that Reno's Italian district was not as clearly defined as those in cities such as Boston, New York, or Philadelphia, and was much smaller; however, most Italian districts in other cities exhibited similarly ill-defined boundaries and contained a variety of ethnic groups.[15]

Reno's small Chinatown had occupied the area around Lake Street between Second Street and the river since the late 1870s. The Chinese neighborhood, populated largely by men who had come into the area doing railroad work and decided to stay, was originally located along First Street between Virginia and Lake streets. The local press viewed Chinatown unfavorably, in keeping with the anti-Chinese prejudice of the time, and used it as a handy scapegoat for any suspicions of disease or criminal activity. The district burned down in 1878 when one William H. Salisbury knocked over a lamp during a fight and started a fire.[16] Chinatown's residents were forced to relocate a little farther east, north of the river between Lake and East (now Record) streets. This placed the heart of Chinatown about two blocks south of the future Lake-Evans block businesses, and established a long-lived Chinese American commercial and residential district.

In 1908, in a move doubtless designed to get rid of Reno's "celestial" population for good, Washoe County ordered that Chinatown's buildings be razed and the remnants burned, on the pretense that the district constituted a health hazard. The county tore down at least sixty buildings, leaving more than one hundred people homeless.[17] While some people did leave, a sizable population stayed, albeit over a slightly more dispersed area, and continued to live and work near downtown.

Chinese American businesses continued operating out of the Lake Street area well into the twentieth century. Longtime Reno resident Harold Curran remembered Chinatown in the 1920s as a small area around Lake and First streets where he could buy firecrackers. A Chinese store owner there, who had moved to Reno from Tonopah, used to give him and his friends Chinese candy at Christmas and let him play with an abacus.[18] Gambling was a popular pastime in this part of town. Local resident Robbins Cahill recalled what the scene was like in the 1920s:

> In those days, there was the old Chinese lottery places. Now it's dignified by the name of "horse race," or Keno, but this was Chinese lottery, played just essentially the same as Keno is played on the same rules today. But you'd go downstairs on Lake Street, between First and Second [and] there were a number of places. Then there was one between Commercial Row and Second. But they were down in the cellar.

Although the lottery was run by the Chinese, Cahill said that it was popular with blacks as well.[19]

It is clear that many different ethnic groups lived and worked together in the area around Lake Street from an early date. Cofone described the "ethnic and social differences" in this part of town as "more a matter of scale than of substance. The greater interaction of different ethnic groups along Lake Street reflected the sociological dynamics of a small western city, as opposed to an eastern metropolitan center."[20]

The first known mention of a business specifically catering to blacks downtown occurred in 1907, when the *Nevada State Journal* reported that the sheriff closed the 400 Club, a "tenderloin negro resort," after a shooting in which William Clark was killed.[21] The club's African American proprietor, Fred Lee, ran his social club on East First Street, in the heart of the Tenderloin. This district, generally centered on East First Street, was roughly bounded by the Truckee River on the south and Second Street on the north, and stretched as far west as Virginia Street and as far east as Evans. The Lake-Evans block north of Second Street seems to have been on the edge of the Tenderloin; while it may not have had the same concentration of brothels and Chinese businesses found in the heart of the district, it definitely had a sprinkling of them. At any rate, according to the *Journal,* the 400 Club had all the trappings of a notorious Tenderloin establishment: "The Black Four Hundred Club is a colored organization, and is noted for the number of fights that take place in the clubrooms every week. Liquor is sold there and white women of the tenderloin [prostitutes] go there and drink, but still no liquor license is paid."[22]

Black-owned clubs were probably present downtown earlier than 1907, and it is possible that Reno had clubs catering to African Americans as early as the 1870s. There is some evidence that the Lake-Evans block housed an African American enclave as early as 1880: eight of Reno's thirty-one African Americans recorded in the 1880 federal census lived in that block.[23] This may be only a coincidence, but it raises the possibility that some of the pre-1930s businesses in the block were owned by blacks. The ReTRAC project focused only on the businesses within the area bounded by Commercial Row, Douglas Alley, Lake Street, and Evans Avenue; the complete history of Reno's black clubs in the Tenderloin and elsewhere has yet to be investigated.

The first known reference to a black club within the Lake-Evans block was in 1924, when the Entertainers Club at the corner of Douglas Alley and Peavine Street was raided by narcotics and Prohibition officers.

Although the race of the owner is unknown, the 28 December *Nevada State Journal* refers to the club as "a rendezvous for colored men."[24] Several more clubs opened in the block during the early 1930s, operating out of "Bottle Alley," a nickname for Douglas Alley. According to newspaper accounts and collaborator interviews, the block was well known as a haven for speakeasies and moonshiners during Prohibition. Some of the speakeasies in the Lake-Evans block even distilled their own moonshine for sale to customers.[25] After Prohibition the clubs became better established, but their public reputation as somewhat seedy purveyors of alcohol lingered, exacerbated by the mainstream white view of this small ethnic enclave.

Douglas Alley and its vicinity had other nicknames as well, including "Peavine Alley," "Skid Row," and "The Row." Clubs in this general area between 1932 and 1977 included the Dixie Club, the Peavine Club, the Club Harlem, the Harlem Club, the Black and Tan Club, the Soul Club and Café, the Top Hat, the China Mint Club, and the New China Club. All of these clubs catered primarily to African Americans and were owned by African or Asian Americans. Patrons accessed the front entrances of the businesses in this block from Douglas Alley rather than Commercial Row, partly because the Virginia & Truckee tracks ran along Commercial and south down Peavine, and partly because alleys were the preferred entries for most of downtown Reno's clubs, restaurants, and bars from at least 1920 to 1960. They were easier for pedestrians to access and were more conducive to social interaction—and in fact became de facto outdoor extensions of the businesses. The ones in the heart of downtown were not dark and dank, as alleys usually are, but brightly lit by the hundreds of bulbs in the signs of the nearby establishments.

Reno's African American population grew slowly in the early twentieth century as African American porters, cooks, and waiters for Southern Pacific opted to move to Reno.[26] Southern Pacific employees on temporary stopovers in town composed part of the visiting black population as well, along with tourists from California who came to Reno for gambling and recreation. The construction of Stead Air Force Base north of Reno and the Sierra Army Depot in Herlong, California, in 1942 led to a much bigger influx of African American men and their families. The bases employed both active-duty military men and civilian workers, and saw their highest populations in the immediate postwar period.

The Dixie Club, located at 218 Douglas Alley, was the earliest con-

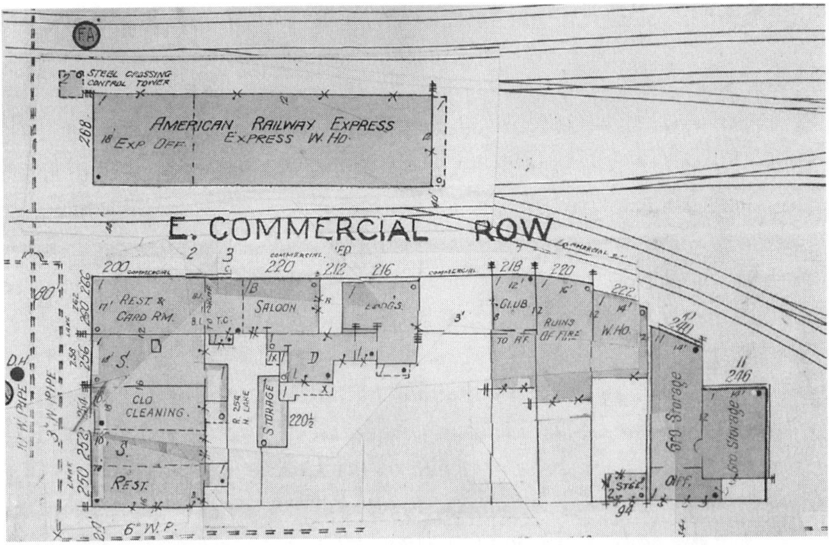


The Dixie Club building as shown on the 1933 Sanborn fire insurance map. Courtesy of the Nevada Historical Society.

firmed African American–owned club in the Lake-Evans block. The first newspaper references to that business that we could find were in 1932, during which year two shootings occurred at the club.[27] Lou LaCou and John Smith were the club's owners at that time.[28] Prohibition officers raided the Dixie Club in January 1933,[29] and local law enforcement kept a close watch on the known speakeasy. After Prohibition was repealed, authorities arrested owner Joe Pureza for selling liquor without a city license; at that time he had owned the Dixie Club for a week and was the first person arrested under the new liquor ordinance.[30] Pureza's ethnic background is not known.

The club did not have a liquor license for a while, and according to a 1933 comment from a representative of the Negro Civic Social Club at a city council meeting, there was nowhere in town for blacks to purchase alcohol.[31] The Dixie Club presumably obtained a license, as it continued in business until 1949; a 1937 advertisement in the *Reno Evening Gazette* notes that the club was under new management, served "home cooked meals and southern fried chicken prepared as only Miss Lena Milton knows how," and had music and floor shows.[32] When owner Elmo Butler died in 1949, the club's lease and belongings were put up for sale.[33] Apparently it never reopened. Not much else is known about the Dixie Club. None of the local residents who shared their memories of the Harlem

Club are old enough to have visited the Dixie Club in its early years, and none remembered what the club was like in its last years in the late 1940s.

The Peavine Club, located at 219 Peavine Street, was established in 1937; a club license was granted in that year to Lucille Woods, Ted Woods, and J. T. Needham.[34] Needham later owned the Dixie Club at 218 Douglas Alley.[35] A 1940 advertisement in the *Reno Evening Gazette* invited people to come to the Peavine Club for Thanksgiving dinner and "Dance to the Best Colored Band in Reno."[36] The Peavine Club apparently closed at some point in the early to middle 1940s, when Bill Bailey applied for a social club bar license and planned to reopen the business as the Club Harlem.[37] The Club Harlem was in operation from 1945 until the summer of 1947, when the city condemned and razed the building at 219 Peavine Street and the establishment moved to 221 Douglas Alley.[38] Bailey's club license was inactive until March 1948, when it was reinstated and he reopened the club at the Douglas Alley location.[39]

The founder of the Harlem Club, William "Bill" Bailey, was born in 1903 in Moreland, Georgia, one of eleven children.[40] According to his biography, in 1917 he lied about his age to enlist in the Illinois National Guard. He fought in World War I and was promoted to sergeant at the age of fifteen. Bailey was wounded twice and spent about a month as a prisoner of war before escaping. He remained in the Army after World

The Harlem Club (Club Harlem), 1967. Note the Chinese lettering on the building to the club's right. Courtesy of the Nevada Historical Society.

War I, working as an instructor, driver, and laborer, then joined the Army Reserves. He moved to Reno in 1934 and started a housecleaning and maintenance business. He ran that business until 1940, then reenlisted in the Army. Bailey served stateside during World War II except for one supply trip to the Pacific Theater, from which he returned escorting Japanese prisoners of war. On that return trip, a restaurant under government contract to feed servicemen refused to serve Bailey because he was black. It gladly served the Japanese POWs.

Moving back to Reno after the war, Bailey bought property at 1518 East Sixth Street and ran it as the Harlem Rooms, a rooming house. He also got into the tavern business and was the owner or part owner of least three clubs: the Peavine Club, the Club Harlem/Harlem Club, and the China Mint Club.[41] Bailey worked as a card dealer at the Dixie Club before becoming part owner of the Peavine Club and later the Harlem Club; in February 1945 he was stabbed in a poker dispute and seriously injured.[42] He continued to work card tables at his later businesses, and newspaper accounts detail more run-ins with disgruntled card players and would-be burglars. In addition to his business dealings, Bailey was a member of the Masonic Order, the Elks Club, the American Woodmen, and the Order of the Eastern Star. He was also president of the Reno-Sparks NAACP and was a prominent community activist specializing in housing discrimination issues. Bailey was a large man in both person and personality; local resident Onie Cooper remembered him as "an outgoing person . . . everyone knew him," and said that he was fond of wearing cowboy boots.[43]

A 12 October 1949 *Nevada State Journal* account of a burglary refers to Bailey's business as the Harlem Club Café.[44] While all of our local collaborators called the club the Harlem Club, a 1967 photograph shows a sign reading "Club Harlem," a probable holdover from the club's original name. The club was popular among the African American airmen based at Stead Air Force Base. The civilian and military residents of Herlong's Sierra Army Depot represented a big portion of its business as well. In fact, onetime Herlong resident Onie Cooper recalled that the Herlong crowd usually outnumbered the Stead crowd at the Harlem Club.[45] In 1955 officials at Stead declared the Harlem Club off limits to its personnel because of allegations of fights, unsanitary conditions, and cases of venereal disease linked to the venue.[46] It seems that not all military personnel obeyed the order, as twenty airmen were arrested at the Harlem Club in a military and civilian police raid there the next year.[47] The base rescinded the order later in 1956.[48]

Bailey became part owner of the China Mint Club in 1958 and was also part owner of the related Happy Buddha Club; his 1960 split from his Chinese American partners in the latter venture was acrimonious.[49] Employee Norval Embry took over the Harlem Club in 1958 and continued operating it at the same location under the same name until 1968, when he renamed it the Soul Club.[50] A white owner briefly ran the Soul Club in 1971, but that sale was overturned when the buyer's business dealings were questioned.[51] In his argument for return of the club to Norval Embry, prominent attorney Charles Kellar, chairman of the western region of the NAACP, stated, "The matter involves the welfare of black people. The owners are the only black people down there and the club has been a black rendezvous for 14 years."[52]

Embry's brother Armster was also a part owner of the Soul Club and took it over when Norval died in a car accident in September 1974 at age sixty-four.[53] Armster Embry had worked as a pit boss at the Harlem Club as early as 1957; according to the *Nevada State Journal,* he was arrested that year after he used obscene language against security officers at Harold's Club, who ejected him because he was black.[54] His wife, Angelina, was also arrested. In court, Embry used his case to argue against the city's "white curtain" of segregation. When the Soul Club ultimately closed in 1977, Embry and his family moved back to Stockton, California.[55]

The last of the clubs to succeed in the Lake-Evans block was Bill Fong's New China Club casino, which fronted on Lake Street. Fong founded the club in 1952, stating that his goal was to establish a club and casino that would cater to African Americans, specifically the airmen based at Stead, as well as all other patrons. The club, which was much larger than the other clubs in the block, was financially successful and openly touted its multiracial patronage. A 1959 *Reno Evening Gazette* advertisement stated that the New China Club would soon double its size—its fifth enlargement in six years: "By summer, we will be the largest interracial casino in the world."[56] The New China Club put on several well-publicized promotions, including inviting Olympian Jesse Owens to crown an African American "Keno Queen" in 1958. Gaming ended at the New China Club on 31 December 1971, when its license expired. Bill Fong had planned to build a new high-rise casino-hotel on the site, but apparently that plan

New China Club advertisement in the *Reno Evening Gazette*, 6 January 1959.

never came to fruition.[57] The building sat unoccupied until it was demolished in the early 1980s.

It is clear that by 1945, the area between Lake and Peavine and north of First Street was well established as the "Negro resort section of Reno."[58] Reno and Sparks did have other African American–owned businesses; they were not all restricted to the Lake-Evans block. Among the best-known clubs were the Dew Drop Inn, originally the Paradise Inn, in Sun Valley; Theresa Elvie King's Green Lantern, east of downtown near the river; and several clubs owned by Earl Perkins, including the Copper Club. There were other black-owned businesses in town besides clubs, of course, including beauty salons, barbershops, rooming houses, shoeshine stands, and restaurants. Before the establishment of several black barbershops, African American women ran informal beauty shops in their houses. Barbers would go from house to house cutting men's hair—local resident Dolores Feemster remembered her children being terrified of the barber and hiding when he came to the door.[59]

Newspaper accounts suggest that city officials evaluated the Lake-Evans businesses using different standards than those used for white establishments. When the Black and Tan Club's club bar license was renewed in January 1946, it was one of only four valid club bar licenses in Reno.[60] At that time there were eighty-seven valid public bar licenses. Club bar licenses allowed alcohol to be served to club members only, while bar licenses allowed service to anyone over the age of twenty-one. The other three club bar licenses were held by the Dixie Club, the Elks Club, and the Club Harlem. Three of those four clubs were located in the Douglas Alley–Peavine Street area and were owned and patronized by blacks. The other, the Elks Club, was a bar in the meeting hall of the Benevolent and Protective Order of Elks.

Most newspaper articles about goings-on in the Lake-Evans block area betray a negative perception of the area's establishments as seedy and rundown. This only served to reinforce the general perception of the clubs as completely distanced from the glittering lights of downtown, despite their location only two blocks away from Virginia Street. Local resident Robbins Cahill described the chasm between black and white in Reno in his 1977 oral history: "That was all part of the early life in Reno, the early structure. The mud was a block and a half away from the center of town, and yet, socially, [and] in every other way, it could've been five miles away, because you cross from one world into another."[61]

Institutionalized racism in Reno continued during the 1940s and 1950s as larger clubs and casinos began flourishing in the downtown core. These businesses did not allow Native American or African American patrons, whether locals or tourists. Some also discriminated against Asian Americans.[62] Even big-name entertainers performing in town were not allowed to eat, lodge, or gamble at the hotel-casinos at which they were headlining. Nevada State Senator Bernice Mathews recalled that when "Sammy Davis Jr. and Louis Armstrong came to Reno, . . . they could not stay in the hotels such as the Mapes and the Riverside in which they played. They had to stay in other places to eat and sleep. They would go to Bill Bailey's Harlem Club and to the New China Club. They would gamble in the New China Club and jam all night in the Harlem Club."[63]

The limited options available to Reno's minority residents created real economic and social hardships. Businesses like the Harlem Club provided not just goods and services, but a safe haven for members of the black community. Both the Dixie Club and the Harlem Club fielded all-black city league baseball teams during the 1940s; the Harlem Club also had a basketball team.[64] It is clear that the Lake-Evans block's businesses served more than one vital purpose during the segregation years.

Local residents Wayne Crawford and Lonnie Feemster told the research team that the block was the center of African American social life well into the 1960s. Crawford said that everyone, even teenagers too young to get into the Harlem Club, would hang out in Douglas Alley and socialize. The older a person got, the closer he could stand to the actual entrance, and the higher his status was among his peers.[65] Oteria Cole also recalled spending a great deal of time at the Harlem Club in the 1950s, and even sneaking in with her friends when she was about fifteen years old. As one of only two black-owned clubs at that particular time—the other was the Dew Drop Inn—the Harlem Club really was the meeting place for African Americans of all ages. "That was home for us, the club was—it was open twenty-four hours."[66] Cole remembered dancing to live music, some by bands that came from California, as well as to jukebox music on the dance floor at the Harlem Club. Onie Cooper remembered that the club was too small for most live acts; its jukebox was the primary draw. He and his friends would grab a bite to eat in the New China Club and then head next door to the Harlem Club to dance.[67]

Vincent Thompson of Bethel African Methodist Episcopal (AME) Church also remembered the music as a big draw for patrons of all ethnicities. In the documentary production *The Black Experience in the Silver State,* he described the Harlem Club as a place where "people met . . . and there were rock and roll bands there, and young white people would come over to the Harlem Club or to some of the parties to listen to the rock and roll."[68] During its heyday in the 1950s and 1960s the Harlem Club contained at various times a bar, dance floor, jukebox, go-go dancer cages, and tables and chairs. After a renovation it connected to Effie May's Café in the adjoining building to the east and served hamburgers and sandwiches.[69] In 1963 a Washoe County Assessor's office map listed the club as occupying three of the "old brick buildings" in that parcel. It is likely that the renovation included the expansion of the club into the adjoining buildings.[70]

The collaboration between Asian and African American business owners in the Lake-Evans block early in the twentieth century is interesting. Charles and Lai King Chew's Cosmo Club, which opened at 142 East Commercial Row, just west of Lake Street, in 1956, was open to African Americans, Native Americans, and Asian Americans.[71] It was one of only two downtown casinos—the New China Club was the other—that explicitly catered to people of all ethnicities. In her oral history Lai King Chew noted that at least one other bar west of Lake Street, the Wagon Wheel Bar, was a "gathering place for colored," and the Aggie Bar was a "gathering place for Indians."[72] The ethnic background of the owners of these clubs is unknown. Chew remembered black patrons being especially fond of craps and keno: "I think their interest in keno stemmed from the fact that in California—Oakland and San Francisco, mostly—the Chinese used to operate keno behind closed doors. . . . It wasn't legal, but they did have keno behind closed doors . . . We had so many keno players in our club that they would stand outside the sidewalk to read the keno board. During the weekend, I would say, we had 98 percent colored people."[73]

Both ethnic groups faced prejudice from the white majority, and it follows that some of their entrepreneurs would band together to do business. Bill Fong and some of the other Chinese American owners of the Happy Buddha, China Mint, Palm, and New China clubs were originally from the San Francisco Bay Area. They founded most of their clubs in Reno to capitalize on tourism from California. The African-Chinese collaboration was also evident in Las Vegas's segregated Westside, where civil rights activist James McMillan recalled "five black gaming joints and two Chinese joints . . . that would hire black people, put them to work."[74] The Chews explored opening a club similar to their Cosmo Club in Westside, but there were already at least two clubs catering to minorities there and they opted to stick to Reno.[75]

Robbins Cahill, a longtime part of the gambling scene in Reno, recalled rumors that white backers financed some of the black clubs in order to keep blacks from coming into the main downtown casinos to gamble.[76] Dolores Feemster and Norma Jean Washington heard a similar rumor circulating about Bill Fong, who operated the integrated New China Club in 1952—the exclusion of African Americans from the big casinos and clubs downtown would have been in his best interest financially.[77] Las Vegas community leader Lubertha Johnson remembered the same thing about the African American club district in her town: "Some type of agreement . . . was made with the power structure that blacks would move to the Westside if they wanted to start their businesses. They would start it on the Westside, but they could not start it downtown."[78]

The Harlem Club/Soul Club was the longest-lived twentieth-century business in the Lake-Evans parcel; it closed in 1977 after twenty-nine years of operation. The building was demolished soon afterward, and the area was paved over. According to local collaborator Wayne Crawford, all of the other old brick buildings housing clubs in the block, except for the one housing the Harlem Club, had already been demolished sometime in the 1950s or 1960s to make room for parking.[79] As mentioned above, the New China Club was torn down in the early 1980s. After that time, the entire block housed a pay parking lot.

Multiple factors caused the decline of the once-busy African American commercial district. Its small, locally owned clubs missed out on the boom of large corporate hotel-casinos that began on Virginia Street in the late 1930s and continued to the north and west during the 1970s–90s. General economic downturns in the 1970s affected all of downtown, as did the decreasing importance of railroad travel; downtown Reno was no longer the central jumping-off point for disembarking travelers.

The Soul Club in 1977, its last year of operation. Courtesy of the Nevada Historical Society.

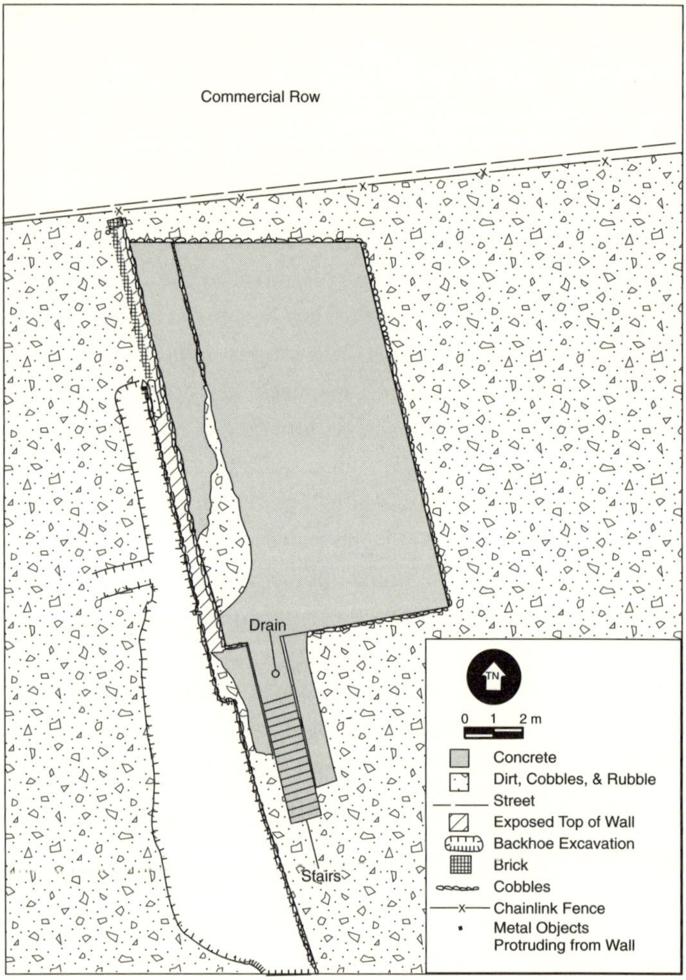


The Harlem Club building's basement (*right*) and the adjoining wall remnant related to the Dixie Club building (*left*). Courtesy of WCRM, Inc.

Prompted partly by improved automobile routes such as Interstate 80 and the city-circumnavigating McCarran Avenue, and partly by a general perception of downtown as a place for tourists rather than locals, many locals moved to new suburban developments on the outskirts of town. This migration further removed the day-to-day lives of residents from the downtown core that once dominated local life. Even long-established businesses in downtown were affected by these changes, and some of them came to be perceived as lower-class establishments because of their location. While the Soul Club survived longer than other businesses in

The partially excavated basement of the Harlem Club building. Courtesy of WCRM, Inc.

the block, eventually it too succumbed to the many changes occurring downtown.

Aside from the causes noted above, the major factor in the decline of the Lake-Evans businesses was desegregation, which began in the mid-1960s. Ironically, the success of the civil rights movement had an unintended adverse economic effect on minority-owned businesses. When African Americans could freely patronize other establishments in addition to the Harlem Club and New China Club, they redistributed the patronage that had once belonged exclusively to those businesses. The same pattern of decline occurred in the African American commercial district in Las Vegas's Westside after the casinos of downtown and the Strip were desegregated. James McMillan pointed out "a downside to integration," noting that "for thirty years after we won our battle I didn't see any construction going on in west Las Vegas."[80] Lubertha Johnson also described mixed feelings about the situation: "You would think that maybe out of loyalty most people would go to the black-owned hotel, but it doesn't work that way. I suppose it's a normal thing . . . It bothers me; it still bothers me a great deal, because I feel that with all the problems and with all of the years of denial, I can't see blacks supporting a group of people who for so long were so partial."[81]

The Cosmo Club also lost most of its business when the Civil Rights Act passed, and Lai King Chew did not renew her lease in 1966. Harrah's bought most of the Commercial Row block between Center and Lake streets, and the rest of the small businesses just west of the Lake-Evans block died.[82]

## ARCHAEOLOGICAL FINDINGS

Because tests of the Harlem Club building's basement found no stratified artifact deposits, we focused on the construction of the basement itself, using a backhoe to expose its interior. The structure was an original component of the brick building constructed at this location sometime between 1899 and 1904. Its north interior wall exhibited a slant just as the historical maps of the aboveground building do, confirming that the structure was angled to accommodate the Virginia & Truckee tracks and that the basement was original to the building rather than a later addition. This wall was built of mortared, faced stone blocks of a uniformly larger size than most of the cobbles in the other walls. From its base, the wall tilted toward the north. It seemed to be thicker at its base and possibly more substantial than the other walls, suggesting additional reinforcement in response to the adjacent railroad tracks. The east interior wall was the least well preserved of the four, having apparently been partially destroyed along with the rest of the standing building in the late 1970s. A concrete-topped ledge ran along most of the basement's west wall. It was constructed of mortared, faced stone, and more closely resembled a storage shelf than a footer or a remnant of an earlier first floor. The dressed cobbles of this shelf were slightly different from those on the basement's main walls, and suggest the ledge may have been a later addition to the original structure. The ledge's southern end terminated in a pronounced curve rather than a right angle.

The basement's south wall contained the brick-framed entrance to a concrete stairwell that led down to the basement from the Douglas Alley–facing entrance. The stairwell opened onto the concrete basement floor through a brick wall vestige with remnants of a wooden doorframe, with its hinge intact. The stairwell was fairly modern in appearance and construction materials, and its concrete walls exhibited poor-quality pouring over older bricks and cobbles. At its top the concrete was fairly friable, and a layer of angular gravels underneath it represented settling of heavier materials due to an overly liquid concrete mix. It is likely that the stairwell was added or renovated by the club's owners during the 1950s or 1960s. The stairs were a private, utilitarian entrance to the building's bottom floor; the main entrance was located above the ground, also in the south end of the building. It is unknown whether this entrance from the outside was an original part of the building, but considering the long history of restaurants, saloons, and clubs here, an exterior entry directly into the basement to facilitate movement and storage of supplies seems likely. It is possible that access to the basement had been closed up at some point, in which case the concrete stairwell could represent a 1950s–60s restoration of access.

The basement's west wall contained a gap in the stones of the masonry wall where an opening of some kind had been filled in with dirt and rubble. No evidence of a formal doorway was found. Two metal objects were also present, protruding eastward and westward from either side of the west wall, partially intersecting the southern edge of the storage ledge. Each object was a thick, two-inch-wide ferrous metal strap running horizontally through/under the wall; on each side of the wall the strap ran through a vertical, round, ferrous metal bar extending upward. The northmost strap extended into the basement's long storage ledge, near its southern end where it curved; this suggests that the metal objects may have predated the ledge. The location of the metal straps, together with the ledge's southern curve and the rubble-filled gap, suggest a passageway here that was filled in at some point. The 1933 Sanborn fire insurance map shows a connection between the club on the left and the "Ruins of Fire" on the right; it is labeled "To R.F." It is tempting to conclude that such a passageway was related to the west building's use as a speakeasy during Prohibition.

We extended and deepened to nine feet a test trench west of the intact basement, in what would have been the basement of the Dixie Club building, to ascertain whether another intact basement was present. The testing showed that no interior wall features or artifact deposits were present, suggesting the Dixie Club building did not have a formal basement in this area.

As there was no filled basement to expose, the rest of the excavation of this area involved extending the trench to the south, all the way to Douglas Alley. The extension revealed an unexpected deep mortar-and-cobble wall that continued well beyond where the southern end of the Dixie Club building would have stood, running south at least as far as the alley. The wall contained multiple components. Its northern portion represented the shared walls of the Harlem Club and Dixie Club buildings. Near the same general area as the metal objects and rubble-filled gap in the west wall of the intact basement described above was a small remnant of an east-west-running wall, possibly representing the southern end of the Dixie Club building's foundation. Just south of here, outside the presumed footprint of the Dixie Club building as shown on the historical maps, the wall extended to a depth of about eight feet—the same as the Harlem Club basement. It then ended, revealing another, older cobble wall running north–south immediately to the east. All of the walls were constructed of uncut native rounded cobbles, not dressed stones like those on the interior of the intact basement.

These walls were intriguing because they suggested an underground connection between the buildings in the northern and southern portions of the parcel. The southern wall lined up with the western edge of one of two conjoined brick buildings constructed between 1890 and 1899, labeled as "female boarding" (a euphemism for brothels or cribs) on the 1899 Sanborn map.[83] The buildings are labeled as dwellings on the 1904

Deep wall extending south of the Harlem Club and Dixie Club buildings. The person to the left is standing on top of the wall, and the stairwell of the Harlem Club basement is in the center-left. Courtesy of WCRM, Inc.

Sanborn map and as "Ruins" on the 1918 Sanborn; they were demolished sometime between 1918 and 1933.[84]

Anyone who has worked in construction in downtown Reno over the last fifty years has heard of secret passageways all over the city. Stories abound of "secret Chinese tunnels" beneath the streets of Reno, ostensibly underground passageways connected to opium dens. Such tunnels are a common myth in western communities, and there is little definitive evidence to link such underground features with the Chinese community or with the opium dens that existed on a much grander scale in the public imagination than in reality. While underground "passageways" in historical buildings are indeed fairly common, they usually represent storage-related facilities associated with commercial buildings. Businesses often shared basement storage space and narrower connecting passages, especially in turn-of-the-century commercial districts where adjoining buildings tended to be constructed in blocks instead of individually. A deceptively tunnel-like storage space discovered next to the 1873 Masonic Hall building on the corner of Sierra Street and Commercial Row (see chapter 3), for example, is a series of narrow basement rooms located directly under the Sierra Street sidewalk. It could easily be misinterpreted as a secret tunnel but in fact served the more prosaic purpose of storing goods for the grocery store occupying the first floor. Such narrow basement vaults are common in nineteenth- and early-twentieth-century buildings, and were accessed directly from the sidewalk via steel doors.

Misinterpretation of basement rooms aside, some of the storied "secret tunnels" downtown may in fact be more than just storage spaces. Lai King Chew told a story about descending to the basement of the Cosmo Club building with a plumber and finding tunnels there. When she asked longtime resident Henry Wu about them, he told her that the tunnels

> were dug to a height of six or seven feet and wide enough for a person to walk through very comfortably. Henry said, "I remember this place. Those tunnels used to be for escapees. When the place was raided for drugs or gambling, people would escape through the tunnel." . . . I don't remember what store it was. I never followed the tunnel all the way, because it was just too spooky. It went all the way under our club, and I presume it went all the way under Douglas Alley, too. . . . All those bars are gone—the hotel, everything.[85]

The deep walls connecting the two sets of buildings in the Lake-Evans block do suggest the presence of an underground passageway; there is no other practical reason to have an underground wall connecting them. The buildings were erected at two different times—the brothel buildings between 1890 and 1899, and the Harlem Club and Dixie Club buildings between 1899 and 1904—and therefore could not have had a built-in underground component resulting from contemporaneous construction. Furthermore, the passageway connecting the Dixie Club and Harlem Club buildings may have been an access point into a longer, deeper hallway or tunnel.

Considering the illicit nature of the two sets of buildings—one a speakeasy, the other a brothel—the prospect of a low-visibility connection is not unreasonable. Most of the town's brothels were located closer to the river, along First Street, and the operation of a brothel so much closer to the center of town and its railroad facilities may have required a little more subtlety. Likewise, any well-established speakeasy or illegal gambling house had a passageway through which a quick exit could be made in case of a police raid. Of course, an equally likely explanation for a connecting passageway is that it was originally used for storage or joint access between two basement storage facilities, and either was expediently used later to escape police raids or had nothing at all to do with the blocks' more notorious activities. Furthermore, the fact that the older southern buildings were labeled "Ruins" in 1918 and were totally removed sometime between 1918 and 1933 argues against much Prohibition-era use of them, unless the ruins were actually used as a hidden entrance/exit. This scenario is almost too romantic to contemplate and is extremely unlikely.

Any further interpretation of "secret tunnels" is largely speculative at this point because of the grand tradition of archaeological bad luck: the research team did not come upon the deeper, older wall until the last day of excavation, and found that it extended beyond the area slated for disturbance within the shoofly right-of-way. For legal reasons we were unable to work outside the proposed area of disturbance or to extend the time frame of the excavation. Because of space limitations related to the restricted area of disturbance, we were unable to trench on the eastern side of the walls to find out what, if anything, lay on the other side of the deep walls. As no further exploration of this southern extension was possible, we cannot definitively say what the deep wall represents.

With a few exceptions, it is clear that the demolition of older buildings to make way for new uses during the 1950s and 1960s severely damaged whatever remained of most of the older buildings in downtown Reno. It also destroyed or removed any intact, stratified deposits of artifacts from earlier times. Though no discrete deposits of historical artifacts were found, the collection of a sample of artifacts from the mixed modern and historical fill provided at least a general idea of the material culture left behind by the Lake-Evans block's residents, business operators, and patrons.

The artifacts found in association with the building features represent a range of items both historical and modern. The assemblage contains at least two gaming implements. One is a plastic Ping-Pong ball bearing a stamp from "The Sports Store"; we could not determine whether this was the manufacturer, wholesaler, or retailer. The ball had been hand-painted with the number "71" to convert it to a keno ball. This suggests that the Harlem Club had a keno operation, although the artifact could also be related to one of the other occupants of the parcel such as the New China Club, which was known to have offered keno. The second gaming piece is a translucent red plastic die with HARLEM CLUB engraved on one side. It confirms that craps or other dice-based games were part of the Harlem Club atmosphere. The presence of the keno ball and Harlem Club die is interesting, as most collaborators remembered gambling being only a minor part of the Harlem Club's social offerings. They recalled a card table but little else. The archaeological evidence indicates the club adopted multiple games over time, perhaps in an attempt to garner more business.

Other artifacts, made of a wide range of materials, include food and beverage service items, entertainment items such as record fragments, and pieces of structural elements from the demolished buildings. Among the miscellaneous artifacts are the remains of a book of matches marked MAMA'S MONEY, manufactured by the Columbia Match Company in Cleveland, Ohio, between 1938 and 1981; part of a plastic tumbler; an earring; bottlecap liners; bottle glass from liquor, beer, and soda bottles dating from the 1930s–70s; pennies (one minted in 1959, one in 1964); a teapot spout; tile fragments; plastic tumblers; lightbulb fragments; and glass tubing from a neon sign. There are eighteen fragments of 45 RPM Columbia label vinyl records containing both paper and etched label fragments showing catalog numbers from the series used between about 1961 and 1963. These record fragments hearken back to a time when the Harlem Club would have been filled with jukebox music and a crowd of dancers.

The artifacts are consistent with the buildings' known mixed usage as clubs with related gaming, music/dancing, liquor, and food service, with some areas used as personal offices, semipublic areas, and a full-time residence. Overall, the artifacts fit with what could reasonably be expected to exist at that location in and before 1977, when the building was demolished. The lack of stratigraphy and the lack of more modern items dating from the 1980s or 1990s support the interpretation that the filling of the basement was a single event that occurred when the above-ground structure was demolished. As discussed earlier, the mixed nature of the deposits limited the amount of information that could be gleaned from artifacts alone. The intact building features themselves proved much more fruitful as windows into the past.

The physical, social, and cultural development of the Lake-Evans block is not only traceable over a one-hundred-plus-year period, it is directly linked to patterns of economic change, evolving perceptions of class, and racial segregation. The block contained an interesting mix of industrial, commercial, and residential occupants, with packing warehouses existing side by side with speakeasies, brothels, and dwellings. Situated close enough to the railroad stations and the main business district to be profitable, but far enough from Virginia Street to be seen as being off the beaten track, the Lake-Evans block was, among other things, a turn-of-the-century nexus for illicit recreation. Its brothels, located adjacent to the main business district rather than in the known red-light district in the Tenderloin to the south, suggest that this block straddled the line between accepted and socially questionable recreation from its early days. Research into the later history of this block confirms that its status as a convenient provider of recreational activities continued well into the twentieth century. As the place to go for liquor during Prohibition, by at least the early 1930s this area was well known as a locus of speakeasies and had a reputation as a rough part of town.

After the repeal of Prohibition and continuing into the 1950s, local African American and Asian American business owners transformed the block into a largely commercial, conventionally recreational destination. As an unsegregated place for African American residents and visitors to gather and socialize during the years when blacks were not allowed in mainstream casinos and clubs, the block contained the most visible ethnic commercial enclave in downtown Reno. At a time when Reno's blacks were denied equal opportunities to buy houses, find work, and patronize local businesses, the enclave provided a valuable service to an underserved community. The block's only partially deserved reputation as a seedy section of town, doubtless exaggerated by widespread racism, continued into the late 1970s, when the last of its businesses shut down.

African and Asian American entrepreneurs established the recreationally oriented businesses of the Lake-Evans block in direct response to the economic, social, and cultural climate of institutionalized racism. The recollections of local informants Oteria Cole, Onie Cooper, Wayne Crawford, Dolores Feemster, Lonnie Feemster, David Love, and Norma Washington reflect fond memories of the Soul Club, the New China Club, and especially the Harlem Club as a home in a hostile environment. These businesses and the others in that one small block were, among other things, physical manifestations of economic and social resistance. Some of them, especially the Harlem Club/Soul Club, survived for a remarkably long time considering the forces arrayed against them. Located in a neglected area of town, subjected to unduly frequent raids and inspections, and serving an underserved and underpaid segment of the population, these clubs nonetheless thrived for years. Until the end of formal segregation greatly diminished the demand for their existence, these establishments were vital social outlets and popular gathering places for Reno's African Americans.

# Conclusion

The enormous casino-hotels that dominate Reno's downtown make it difficult to envision a landscape of shorter brick buildings and neon-lit alleyways, let alone the wood-framed structures that mushroomed from the valley floor in 1868 or the low, rounded houses that sat by the river in prehistoric times. Before work began on the ReTRAC project, no large archaeological projects had been conducted within the Reno city limits; as a result, many people were surprised to find that the remnants of many years of human occupation survived beneath the modern streetscape. Reno is too often viewed not as a real place with a real past, but as a tourists' playground without much in the way of physical permanence and with a demonstrated knack for destroying the old to make way for the new.

The first earth-disturbing activities on the ReTRAC project proved that the opposite is true: despite the years of demolition, construction, and utility maintenance, and despite the thoroughly modern appearance of Reno's downtown core, many archaeological resources survive below the ground surface. Certainly there have been significant disturbances to parts of downtown; as demonstrated by many of the historical sites discovered during the project, utility work and large-scale construction did destroy some of Reno's archaeological record. But enough physical remnants of the city's history survive to enable extensive investigations into the people of the region's past. Oddly enough, the best-preserved site was by far the oldest—covered by hundreds of years' worth of soft stream terrace sediments and capped by the Central Pacific railroad bed in 1868, the prehistoric Daylight site was in better shape than any of the twentieth-century sites we examined. The very thing that created modern Reno—the transcontinental railroad—inadvertently preserved this ancient site.

The archaeological sites under the urban setting of modern Reno contain many stories about the people who left them there, and only a few of those stories are told here. Much more remains to be learned and shared about those who lived in this riverside location in Nevada's high desert. Even these few sites, though, show that there was much more to the American West than is popularly imagined. In this quintessential western landscape, Native American children played in the willows next to the river as their mothers ground seeds. Later inhabitants struggled to provide clean drinking water for their families and picked themselves up after a series of devastating fires. Italian workmen dug a tunnel under the railroad tracks in the first attempt to solve the problems associated with an active rail line through the middle of the city. Two Jewish brothers kept their bottling works running during Prohibition. African American club owners provided a home away from home for blacks who faced

Looking east toward Reno and the newly built railroad, 1868. Photo by Joseph M. Graham of the Central Pacific Railroad. Courtesy of Department of Special Collections and University Archives, Stanford University Libraries.

Looking east toward Reno and the railroad main line, taken from the same location, 1997. Photo by Lawrence K. Hersh, from *The Central Pacific Railroad across Nevada 1868 & 1997* (2000), used by permission.

daily discrimination. All of the stories paint a picture of a past more complex and multidimensional than Reno's history is usually thought to be.

The vast majority of the people who have ever lived are either underrepresented in the historical record or not represented at all. The occupants of the Truckee Meadows prior to the early 1840s had no written language. Theirs was an oral tradition, and although much has been learned from the keepers of that tradition, the only other way to know them is to study the little pieces of the puzzle that they left behind. With these fragments, at least a partial picture of who they were can be constructed. There is strong archaeological evidence of human occupation of the Truckee Meadows for the past 5,000 years, but people have almost certainly been here longer. The presence of Clovis projectile points in Washoe Valley, only twenty miles to the south, suggests that humans were in this area as early as 12,000 years ago. The Daylight site proves that there are deeply buried, stratified sites in the Truckee Meadows. The 7,600-year-old Mazama ash layer found about twelve feet below the present street level in downtown Reno confirmed the presence of deeply buried sediments in this area. It is likely that evidence of even older occupations awaits discovery elsewhere in the valley, quite probably along the Truckee River.

In later times Reno was an urban center with an ethnically diverse population consisting of many more people whose lives never made it into the written record. Archaeology provides a vital avenue for attempts to re-create their everyday lives. In fleshing out the reality of past lives in the West, a more complete picture emerges of a region that was more than a wild and lawless frontier—it was also a place of urbanity, diversity, and, of course, humanity.

People's relationships with place are often expressed through the concept of kinship: the land as a mother, a childhood home as a member of the family. When Reno demolished the Mapes Hotel, a locally beloved building, many residents mourned the loss as if it were a death. The physical environment provides a constant reminder of the ties between present and past, promoting a feeling of being rooted in a place. But as discussed in this book and others, Reno's landscape has changed dramatically in the past sixty years, and many of the buildings and features that provide connections with history have been obliterated.

In her 2008 book *Reno's Big Gamble,* historian Alicia Barber described Reno's identity as being composed of three elements: sense of place, promoted image, and civic reputation.[1] The sense of place is personal and subjective, essentially boiling down to how residents feel about their city. The promoted image is aspirational and idealistic, usually manufactured by city leaders. Civic reputation is the unruly result of both inner and outer perceptions, or as Barber asserted, "a product of rampant public discussion rather than individual reflection or tightly focused market research."[2] These three components "can resemble each other closely or differ drastically, but all depend fundamentally upon the final factor in the matrix of place identity, the place itself. As the most tangible component in this equation, the physical place is ultimately prone to the most permanent alteration in the quest to improve a city's reputation."[3]

Over the years, Reno defined and redefined itself in a never-ending quest for survival, and until very recently kept its focus on the tourist market. In the process the city sacrificed most of its downtown core. Reno earned, intentionally or not, a civic reputation as a town of transients—a place to visit or a temporary stopping point on the way to someplace else. This perception began in the city's early years of development, when the valley was, as historian John M. Townley put it, "an exploitable market for goods and services to most of its residents, who hoped to retire to California with their earnings."[4] In the early twentieth century Reno became a unique destination for people seeking divorce; the six-month—and, later, six-week—residency requirement resulted in a constantly shifting and renewing population of temporary residents. When gambling laws were relaxed and casinos began to grow, the population of temporary recreation seekers increased, and the resulting jobs attracted an only slightly more anchored population of service and gaming workers. In the mid-to-late twentieth century, corporations bulldozed older buildings in order to construct enormous casino-hotels, and residents more or less avoided downtown.

Meanwhile, out of the spotlight, Reno's permanent population grew steadily; many of those once-temporary workers stayed and raised families. Native American residents whose families had lived in the area for many generations continued to make their homes on the land. Locals worked for improvements in infrastructure, economic opportunity, and community involvement, and Reno flourished as a result. Despite continuous urban growth and a well-established permanent population, the general public perception of Reno as a city where most people are "just passing through" has persisted. This perception is not entirely inaccurate—its reliance on tourist dollars and the resultant influence on the highly visible downtown area have made Reno what it is today. However, the people who really made Reno what it is are those who stayed over the long term.

The rise of other gambling options, namely Las Vegas and California's Indian casinos, has significantly affected Reno's economy and has forced its leaders to start looking inward. In the past few years Reno has adopted a new redefinition as a recreational destination, appealing to locals as well as tourists. The revitalization of the river corridor has led to an influx of small, locally owned businesses and the return of locals to downtown, at least for eating, drinking, and shopping. Developers have started to add residential space back to the downtown core in the form of condominium complexes, many rebuilt from the skeletons of bankrupt casino-hotels. The city council approved Reno's first Historic Plan in 2008, taking a promising step toward establishing a stronger framework for protecting cultural resources. All of these changes may eventually lead Reno's civic reputation, promoted image, and sense of place to converge.

These positive developments notwithstanding, the demolition of Reno's historical landscape shows no sign of slowing. At the time of this writing, the city is planning to replace the historic Virginia Street Bridge, built in 1905. The 1873 Masonic building at the corner of Commercial Row and Sierra Street is privately owned by a corporation considering construction of a luxury boutique hotel on the block. The owner's plans for the oldest standing commercial building in Reno are unknown. Development projects, some involving an enormous amount of ground disturbance, take place with little or no archaeological monitoring or research. The construction of the baseball stadium is the latest example. The results of the ReTRAC project prove that a great deal of Reno's archaeological record survives beneath the ground surface. This record is as important as the structures that stand atop the ground surface, and it deserves some consideration as the city plans its future.

Reno is more than its physical location and built landscape. It is the sum of many stories and experiences, all tied together and reaching from the past into the present. Archaeologist Julian Thomas said that our personal stories are built up from located acts.[5] So, too, is the biography of Reno constructed from the thousands of lives that have been lived here. In 1941 journalist Max Miller published *Reno,* a mix of fact and fiction that includes this snapshot of the paradox that is Reno:

> I certainly remember my first impression, so was not surprised, for I also had been told ahead of time that "this would be Reno." My surprise came later when on walking west from downtown, when on walking along the Truckee, I saw a new town entirely. But it was still Reno, the bigger Reno, the Reno which causes the citizens to live their whole lives here and to love their town.
>
> The mountain river bank above the business section is all one continuous park lined by homes and more homes and still more homes. Mallard ducks, free and unclipped, live upon the river and have their nests upon the river banks. If you sit upon a rock there the ducks will swim up to you to be fed from your hands, or merely to talk with you in their own language, or to show off their fleet of newly hatched ducklings to you. And boys and men will be fishing the Truckee right alongside the bridges in the heart of town. One can fish for trout from his own windows almost, and always in the background like a great drop-curtain shielding Reno from the ordinary world is the High Sierra, peak after peak with pockets of snow, with pines, with brazen boulders. And this is the real Reno which gets into the heart of one, more the name of a region than of a town,

so that the hurdy-gurdy of the gambling section becomes a minute speck indeed, an incident used for meeting trains.

Instead of Reno becoming smaller with intimacy as the days go along, Reno for a fact spreads and enlarges in focus. And this, I think, all this intangible mystery, all this gradual unfolding, is why people return.[6]

Research into the past of this small western city has proved Miller's assertion true: the more we learn about Reno, the more it seems to spread and enlarge, unfolding gradually. This is true of almost any place; delving into history and searching for the reality under the popular image seems to result in as many questions as answers. The past is a complicated place. If these few stories of Reno's historical occupants prove anything, it is that this past is worth preserving.

# Notes

## ABBREVIATIONS FOR FREQUENTLY CITED SOURCES

| | |
|---|---|
| *CA* | *Carson (Daily) Appeal* |
| *GHN* | *Gold Hill (Daily) News* |
| *NHSQ* | *Nevada Historical Society Quarterly* |
| *NSJ* | *Nevada State Journal* (Reno) |
| *REG* | *Reno Evening Gazette* |
| *RWG* | *Reno Weekly Gazette* |
| *ST* | *Sparks Tribune* |

### INTRODUCTION

1. These mandates are set forth in the Antiquities Act of 1906, the National Historic Preservation Act of 1966 (as amended), the National Environmental Policy Act of 1974, and the Archaeological Resources Protection Act of 1979.

2. Julian Thomas, "Archaeologies of Place and Landscape," in *Archaeological Theory Today* (Bristol: Policy Press, 2001), 173.

### 1 | A BRIEF HISTORY OF RENO

1. Gordon R. Willey and Philip Phillips, *Method and Theory in American Archaeology* (Chicago: University of Chicago Press, 1958), 22.

2. Robert G. Elston, "Good Times, Hard Times: Prehistoric Culture Change in the Western Great Basin," in *Man and Environment in the Great Basin*, SAA Papers 2, ed. David B. Madsen and James F. O'Connell (Washington, DC: Society for American Archaeology, 1982), 189.

3. Ibid., 196; Charles D. Zeier and Robert G. Elston, eds., *The Archaeology of the Vista Site 26Wa3017*, report submitted to Cultural Resources Section, Environmental Services Division, of the Nevada Department of Transportation, Carson City (Silver City, NV: Intermountain Research, 1986).

4. Elston, "Good Times, Hard Times," 199.

5. Zeier and Elston, *The Archaeology of the Vista Site*, 377–79.

6. Grace Dangberg, *Washo Tales: Three Original Washo Legends*, Occasional Papers of the Nevada State Museum (Carson City: Nevada State Museum, 1968), 1; Julian H. Steward, "Linguistic Distribution and Political Groups of the Great Basin Shoshoneans," *American Anthropologist* 39, no. 4 (1937): 625–34; Warren L. d'Azevedo, "Comments on Tribal Distribution," in *The Current Status of Anthropological Research in the Great Basin 1964*, Social Sciences and Humanities Publication 1, Technical Report Series S-H, ed. Warren L. d'Azevedo, Wilbur A. Davis, Don D. Fowler, and Wayne Shuttles (Reno: Desert Research Institute, in cooperation with the Department of

Anthropology and the Center for Western North American Studies, University of Nevada, 1966), 315–34; Alfred L. Kroeber, *Handbook of the Indians of California* (New York: Dover, 1976; reprint of Bulletin 78 of the Bureau of American Ethnology of the Smithsonian Institute, 1925), 571.

7. Inter-Tribal Council of Nevada, Reno, *Numa: A Northern Paiute History* (Reno: Inter-Tribal Council of Nevada, printed by the University of Utah Printing Service, Salt Lake City, 1976), 1.

8. Sydney Lamb, "Linguistic Prehistory in the Great Basin," *International Journal of American Linguistics* 24, no. 2 (1958): 95–100; Robert G. Elston, "How Will I Know You? Archaeological Visibility of the Numic Spread in the Western Great Basin," in *Across the West: Human Population Movement and the Expansion of the Numa,* ed. David B. Madsen and David Rhode (Salt Lake City: University of Utah Press, 1994), 150–51; David B. Madsen and David Rhode, introduction to *Across the West: Population Movement and the Expansion of the Numa,* 3–5.

9. Grace Dangberg, Field Notes, File IV/1 (no date), 48, in The Records of John A. Price (Collection no. 99-20), University of Nevada, Reno, Special Collections, 1961–88.

10. Warren L. d'Azevedo, "Ethnohistorical Notes on Eagle Valley, Carson City, Nevada," appendix 2 in *The Archaeology of the Stewart Dump Site (26Or121),* Nevada State Museum Archaeological Services Report 13, no. 2, by Eugene M. Hattori (Carson City: Nevada State Museum, 1978), 69–75.

11. Kroeber, *Handbook of the Indians of California,* 570; Dangberg, Field Notes, 48.

12. Catherine S. Fowler, comp. and ed., *Willard Z. Park's Ethnographic Notes on the Northern Paiute of Western Nevada, 1933–1944,* University of Utah Anthropological Papers 114 (Salt Lake City: University of Utah, 1989), 5.

13. Inter-Tribal Council of Nevada, *Wa She Shu: A Washo Tribal History* (Reno: Inter-Tribal Council of Nevada, 1976), 77.

14. Robert R. Kautz, "Modeling Precontact Lifeways in the Truckee Meadows" (paper presented at the 28th Annual Conference of the Nevada Archaeological Association, Reno, NV, March 1999); Edward J. Stoner and Mary K. Rusco, *A pá wa detdé' yi' Village: The Archaeology of the Sunridge Site (26Do439) Douglas County, Nevada* (Sparks, NV: Western Cultural Resource Management, 2001); Warren L. d'Azevedo, "Washoe," in *Handbook of North American Indians,* vol. 11: *Great Basin,* ed. Warren L. d'Azevedo (Washington, DC: Smithsonian Institution, 1986), 466–98.

15. Inter-Tribal Council of Nevada, *Wa She Shu,* 75.

16. Catherine S. Fowler, "Subsistence," in *Handbook of North American Indians,* vol. 11: *Great Basin,* ed. Warren L. d'Azevedo (Washington, DC: Smithsonian Institution, 1986), 87.

17. Kenneth L. Holmes, *Covered Wagon Women. Diaries & Letters from the Western Trails, 1852,* vol. 4: *The California Trail* (Lincoln, NE: Bison Books and University of Nebraska Press, 1997), 160.

18. Fowler, *Willard Z. Park's Ethnographic Notes on the Northern Paiute of Western Nevada, 1933–1944,* 50.

19. Robert M. Lanner, *The Pinon Pine: A Natural and Cultural History* (Reno: University of Nevada Press, 1981); Inter-Tribal Council of Nevada, *Wa She Shu,* and *Numa.*

20. Fowler, *Willard Z. Park's Ethnographic Notes on the Northern Paiute of Western Nevada, 1933–1944,* 5.

21. Stanley A. Freed and Ruth S. Freed, "The Persistence of Aboriginal Ceremonies among the Washo Indians," in *The Washo Indians of California and Nevada,* Anthropological Papers 67 (Salt Lake City: Department of Anthropology, University of Utah, 1963), 34.

22. Lanner, *The Pinon Pine,* 79.

23. Richard O. Clemmer and Omer C. Stewart, "Treaties, Reservations and Claims," in *Handbook of North American Indians,* vol. 11: *Great Basin,* ed. Warren L. d'Azevedo (Washington, DC: Smithsonian Institution, 1986), 536; Inter-Tribal Council of Nevada, *Numa.*

24. Clemmer and Stewart, "Treaties, Reservations and Claims," 538.

25. Ibid., 539.

26. Eugene M. Hattori, *Northern Paiutes on the Comstock: Archaeology and Ethnohistory of an American Indian Population in Virginia City, Nevada,* Nevada State Museum Occasional Papers 2 (Carson City: Nevada State Museum, 1975), 19, 23.

27. Clemmer and Stewart, "Treaties, Reservations and Claims," 539.

28. Edwin Bryant, *What I Saw in California* (1849; reprint, Palo Alto, CA: Lewis Osborne, 1967), 224.

29. John M. Townley, *Tough Little Town on the Truckee* (Reno: Great Basin Studies Center, 1983), 44.

30. Mella Rothwell Harmon, "Land Development and the Railroad in Nineteenth Century Reno" (paper presented at the Nevada Historical Society, Reno, October 2007), 8.

31. Doris Cerveri, *Reno: A Pictorial History* (Norfolk, VA: Donning Company, 1981), 17, in Susan Stornetta, Thomas D. Burke, Ronald L. Reno, Vickie L. Clay, and C. Lynn Furnis, *Reno Railroad Corridor: Archaeological Resources Technical Report,* prepared for Myra L. Frank and Associates, Inc., Los Angeles (Virginia City, NV: Archaeological Research Services, 2000), 2.12; Townley, *Tough Little Town on the Truckee,* 53.

32. Phillip I. Earl, "Notes and Documents: Meandering along the Line of the Central Pacific Railroad, 1868," *NHSQ* 21, no. 4 (1978): 281–82.

33. Townley, *Tough Little Town on the Truckee,* 73.

34. Bertha Bender Brown, *A Tale of Three Cities: Reno, Carson, San Francisco: 1863–1930* (Healdsburg, CA: Naturegraph Publishers, 1964), 44.

35. Stornetta et al., *Reno Railroad Corridor,* 3.22.

36. Ibid.

37. Wilbur S. Shepperson, *Restless Strangers: Nevada's Immigrants and Their Interpreters,* Nevada and the West, Lancehead Series (Reno: University of Nevada Press, 1970), 185, 205, in Stornetta et al., *Reno Railroad Corridor,* 3.23.

38. Some sources state that six people died: Townley, *Tough Little Town on the Truckee*; Peggy Trego, "1879 Brought Death and Destruction to Little Reno," *NSJ* 25

February 1951, 3. Others say five: *REG,* 2 March 1880, 2; Reno Fire Department, *History of the Reno Fire Department* (Reno: Firemen's Pension and Relief Fund, 1908). All agree that Mrs. John "Mother" Beck, Joseph Kilpatrick, John Irvin, Joseph Pailan or Philan (the primary account with his name in it, *NSJ,* 7 March 1879, 3, is barely legible), and an "unidentified Indian" were killed. The unidentified body was found burned beyond recognition in the ruins of the State Flouring Mills and was identified as Native American using a questionable nineteenth-century morphological exercise: "The skull and other anatomical peculiarities led to the conclusion that it was an Indian" (*RWG,* 6 March 1879, 5). The sixth fatality was popular bartender Joe Crews, who was badly burned in the fire and died of his injuries several days later. The fact that he died later probably accounts for his initial exclusion from the casualty count; he was not listed among the known dead until more than a week after the fire (*RWG,* 6 March 1879, 5). His funeral was on 12 March 1879 (*REG,* 12 March 1879, 3).

39. Stornetta et al., *Reno Railroad Corridor,* 2.20, 2.22–23.

40. Nevada Division of Water Resources, *Truckee River Chronology: A Chronological History of Lake Tahoe and the Truckee River and Related Water Issues,* Nevada Water Basin Information and Chronology Series (Carson City: Nevada Division of Water Resources, 1997), http://water.nv.gov/WaterPlanning/truckee/trchrono.cfm

41. Ibid.

42. William D. Rowley, *Reno: Hub of the Washoe Country* (Woodland Hills, CA: Windsor Publications, 1984), 36–37.

43. Ibid., 22.

44. Ibid., 31.

45. For an excellent examination of the divorce trade in Reno and its influence on the local economy, see Mella Rothwell Harmon, "Divorce and Economic Opportunity in Reno, Nevada during the Great Depression" (master's thesis, University of Nevada, Reno, 1998).

46. Rowley, *Reno: Hub of the Washoe Country,* 31.

47. Ibid., 37.

48. Max Miller, *Reno* (New York: Dodd, Mead, 1941), 25.

49. Barbara Land and Myrick Land, *A Short History of Reno* (Reno: University of Nevada Press, 1995), 104, in Paul F. Starrs, Heather Van Wormer, and Jeanne Harrah, *Downtown Reno and the Railroad,* Report to the Surface Transportation Board, Section for Environmental Analysis; "Historical Development and Growth of Downtown Reno Project" (Reno, 1997), 20.

50. Land and Land, *A Short History of Reno,* 105, in Starrs et al., *Downtown Reno and the Railroad,* 20.

51. Nevada Division of Water Resources, *Truckee River Chronology.*

52. Starrs et al., *Downtown Reno and the Railroad.*

## 2 | OCCUPANTS OF THE DAYLIGHT SITE

1. L. V. Benson, D. R. Currey, R. I. Dorn, K. R. Lajoie, C. G. Oviatt, S. W. Robinson, G. I. Smith, and S. Stine, "Chronology of Expansion and Contraction of Four

Great Basin Lake Systems during the Past 35,000 Years," *Paleogeography, Paleoclimatology, Paleoecology* 78 (1990): 241–86. During much of the late Pleistocene (ca. 126,000–10,000 years ago) much of northwestern Nevada was covered by a huge pluvial (glacial-fed) lake known as Lake Lahontan. The lake reached its maximum extent, or "high stand," about 15,000 years ago.

2. Donald K. Grayson, *The Desert's Past* (Washington, DC: Smithsonian Institution Press, 1993); Peter E. Wigand and David Rhode, "Great Basin Vegetation History and Aquatic Systems: The Last 150,000 Years," In *Great Basin Aquatic Systems History,* Smithsonian Contributions to Earth Sciences 33, ed. R. Hershler, David B. Madsen, and D. R. Currey (Washington, DC: Smithsonian Institution Press, 2002), 309–67.

3. For more information on absolute dating methods, see Sheridan Bowman, *Interpreting the Past: Radiocarbon Dating* (Berkeley: University of California Press, 1990).

4. Robert G. Elston, Susan Stornetta, Daniel P. Dugas, and Peter Mires, "Beyond the Blue Roof: Archaeological Survey of the Mt. Rose Fan and Northern Steamboat Hills," submitted to the USDA Forest Service, Toiyabe National Forest, Sparks, NV (Silver City, NV: Intermountain Research, 1994); see Charles D. Zeier and Robert G. Elston, eds., *Changes in Washoe Land Use Patterns: A Study of Three Archaeological Sites in Diamond Valley, Alpine County, California,* Monographs in World Archaeology 5 (Madison, WI: Prehistory Press, 1992); Robert G. Elston, "Prehistory of the Western Area," in *Handbook of North American Indians,* vol. 11: *Great Basin,* ed. Warren L. d'Azevedo (Washington, DC: Smithsonian Institution, 1986), 135–48.

5. Elston, "Prehistory of the Western Area."

6. Steven R. Simms, *Ancient Peoples of the Great Basin and Colorado Plateau* (Walnut Creek, CA: Left Coast Press, 2008), 26.

7. Grayson, *The Desert's Past*; Wigand and Rhode, "Great Basin Vegetation History and Aquatic Systems."

8. David H. Thomas, *The Archaeology of Monitor Valley, 1: Epistemology,* Anthropological Papers of the American Museum of Natural History 59, no. 1 (1983); Robert G. Elston and Elizabeth E. Budy, "Research Perspectives," in *The Archaeology of James Creek Shelter,* ed. Robert G. Elston and Elizabeth E. Budy, University of Utah Anthropological Papers 115 (1990): 9–24; Elston et al., "Beyond the Blue Roof"; Alan R. Schroedl, *Excavations in the North Block Tailings Impoundment Area, North Central Nevada* (Salt Lake City: P-III Associates, 1996); Kelly R. McGuire, Michael G. Delacorte, and Kimberly Carpenter, *Archeological Excavations at Pie Creek and Tule Valley Shelters, Elko County, Nevada,* Nevada State Museum Anthropological Papers 25 (Carson City: Nevada State Museum, 2004); Kelly R. McGuire and William R. Hildebrandt, "Re-thinking Great Basin Foragers: Prestige Hunting and Costly Signaling during the Middle Archaic Period," *American Antiquity* 70, no. 4 (2005): 695–712.

9. James F. O'Connell and Kristen Hawkes, "Alyawara Plant Use and Optimal Foraging Theory," in *Hunter Gatherer Foraging Strategies,* ed. Bruce Winterhalder and Eric A. Smith (Chicago: University of Chicago Press, 1981), 99–125; Steven R. Simms, "The Evolution of Hunter-Gatherer Foraging Strategies" (paper presented at the Society for American Archaeology meeting in Pittsburg, PA, 1983); David R. Yesner,

"Life in the 'Garden of Eden': Causes and Consequences of the Adoption of Marine Diets by Human Societies," in *Food and Evolution,* ed. Marvin Harris and Eric B. Ross (Philadelphia: Temple University Press, 1989), 285–310.

10. McGuire et al., *Archeological Excavations at Pie Creek and Tule Valley Shelters, Elko County, Nevada*; McGuire and Hildebrandt, "Re-thinking Great Basin Foragers."

11. Elston, "How Will I Know You?"

12. James F. Downs, *Washoe Religion,* University of California Anthropological Records 16, no. 9 (1961): 365–85; d'Azevedo, "Washoe."

13. David W. Zeanah, "Sexual Division of Labor and Central Place Foraging: a Model for the Carson Desert of Western Nevada," *Journal of Anthropological Archaeology* 23 (2004): 1–32.

14. Jonathan O. Davis, "Bits and Pieces: The Last 35,000 Years in the Lahontan Area," in *Man and Environment in the Great Basin,* ed. David B. Madsen and James F. O'Connell, Society for American Archaeology Papers 2 (Washington, DC: Society for American Archaeology, 1982), 53–75; Peter E. Wigand, "Diamond Pond, Harney County, Oregon: Vegetation History and Water Table in the Eastern Oregon Desert," *Great Basin Naturalist* 47 (1987): 427–58; Peter E. Wigand and C. L. Nowak, "Dynamics of Northwest Nevada Plant Communities during the Last 30,000 Years," in *The History of Water: Eastern Sierra Nevada, Owens Valley, White-Inyo Mountains,* White Mountain Research Station Symposium 4, ed. C. A. Hall, V. Doyle-Jones, and B. Widawski (Los Angeles: University of California, 1992), 40–62; Peter E. Wigand and Martin R. Rose, "Calibration of High Frequency Pollen Sequences and Tree-Ring Records," *Proceedings of the International Highlevel Radioactive Waste Management Conference and Exposition,* Las Vegas, NV, 1990.

15. Wigand and Rhode, "Great Basin Vegetation History and Aquatic Systems," fig. 11.

16. Robert G. Elston and Jonathan O. Davis, "An Investigation of the Steamboat Hot Springs Locality, Washoe County, Nevada," *Nevada Archaeological Survey Reporter* 6, no. 1 (1972): 9–14; Robert G. Elston, "The Archaeology of U.S. 395 Right-of-Way between Stead, Nevada and Hallelujah Junction, California," submitted to the California Department of Transportation (University of Nevada Archeological Survey, 1979), manuscript on file in Special Collections, University of Nevada, Reno.

17. Peter E. Wigand, "Modern and Late Holocene Ecology of Northwestern Nevada," appendix 10 in *The Archaeology of "The Biggest Little City in the World": The ReTRAC Project, Reno, Washoe County, Nevada: Prehistoric Resources,* ed. Edward J. Stoner, Mary Ringhoff, Robert R. Peterson, and Jennifer Sigler (Sparks, NV: Western Cultural Resource Management, 2006).

18. Once we determined the Daylight site remains to be prehistoric, Nevada Revised Statute (NRS) 383.170 required the immediate notification of the State Historic Preservation Office (SHPO). The SHPO notified the tribes, and a plan was developed to address the remains and any human remains subsequently found during excavation of the site. In this case the Nevada state laws governing Indian burials, NRS 383.150–383.190, superseded federal law, including the North American Grave

Protection and Repatriation Act (NAGPRA), because the Daylight site was located on privately owned land. NRS 383.170 c. states that upon written consent of the tribes, the remains and any associated artifacts shall be excavated and that "all artifacts and human remains removed during such an excavation, must, after scientific study, be reinterred under the supervision of the Indian Tribe." Nevada Revised Statutes, "Protection of Indian Burial Sites, NRS 383.150–383.170" (Carson City: State of Nevada Printing Office, 1994).

19. Margaret M. Rucks, "The Social Context and Cultural Meaning of Ground Stone Milling among Washoe Women" (master's thesis, University of Nevada, Reno, 1995), 86–87.

20. Margaret M. Rucks, "World View as a Site Formation Process: Ground Stone Milling by Washoe Women," unpublished, undated manuscript, 11.

21. Stanley A. Freed and Ruth S. Freed, "A Confirmation of Aboriginal Washo Culture," in *The Washo Indians of California and Nevada*, Anthropological Papers 67 (Salt Lake City: University of Utah Department of Anthropology, 1963), 49.

22. Ibid., 50.

23. Rucks, "The Social Context and Cultural Meaning of Ground Stone Milling among Washoe Women," 91.

## 3 | RENO AND THE RAILROAD

1. Nan A. Rothschild and Diana diZerega Rockman, "Method in Urban Archaeology: The Stadt Huys Block," in *Archaeology of Urban America: The Search for Pattern and Process*, ed. Roy S. Dickens Jr. (New York: Academic Press, 1982), 4.

2. *GHN*, 22 July 1868, 2.

3. Starrs et al., *Downtown Reno and the Railroad*, i.

4. Ibid., 16.

5. Ibid., 4.

6. Ibid., 3.

7. [no first name given] Drake, *Reno, Washoe County, Nevada*, map, revised January 1901 by E. P. (Nevada Historical Society, Reno), in Stornetta et al., *Reno Railroad Corridor*, 2.15.

8. Ibid.

9. National Park Service, "How to Apply the National Register Criteria for Evaluation," *National Register Bulletin* 15 (Washington, DC: National Park Service, 1991), 53.

10. Hans and April Halberstadt, *The American Train Depot and Roundhouse* (Osceola, WI: Motorbooks International, 1995), 50–53.

11. Ibid., 50.

12. *NSJ*, 20 August 1873, 1.

13. Kelly J. Dixon, *Boomtown Saloons: Archaeoloogy and History in Virginia City* (Reno: University of Nevada Press, 2005), 93–94.

14. *RWG*, 13 March 1879, 8.

15. Phillip I. Earl, "Reno's Southern Pacific Depot Has Historic Significance," *North Lake Tahoe Bonanza*, 11 October 1991, 17.

16. *NSJ*, 14 February 1877, 1.17. *NSJ*, 24 January 1954, 6.

17. *NSJ*, 24 January 1954, 6.

18. T. B. Camp, *Reno, Nevada,* map, December 1879, Nevada Historical Society, Reno.

19. *NSJ*, 14 January 1882, 1.

20. *NSJ*, 24 January 1954, 6.

21. Sanborn Map and Publishing Company, *Reno, Nev. April 1890,* fire insurance map (New York: Sanborn Map and Publishing Company, 1890).

22. Sanborn Map and Publishing Company, *Reno, Nev. May 1904,* fire insurance map (New York: Sanborn Map and Publishing Company, 1904).

23. *REG*, 18 June 1913, 1.

24. *REG*, 3 October 1910, 1.

25. *ST*, 5 June 1925, 1.

26. The three buildings were recorded and nominated to the Register in 1983 as part of an architectural survey of Reno. Gail Miller and Rick Starzak, Historic Resources Inventory Form for the Southern Pacific Railroad Passenger Station (Amtrak Depot), 1999, in Myra L. Frank & Associates, Inc., Request for Determination of Eligibility for the Reno Railroad Corridor, City of Reno, Washoe County, Nevada, prepared by Myra L. Frank & Associates, Inc., for the Federal Highway Administration, the Nevada Department of Transportation, and the City of Reno, Nevada, 2000.

27. Norman Tyler, *Historic Preservation: An Introduction to Its History, Principles, and Practice* (New York: W. W. Norton, 2000), 15.

28. *NSJ*, 18 March 1902, 1.

29. *NSJ*, 7 November 1902, 1; 8 November 1902, 1.

30. *REG*, 7 November 1902, 6.

31. *REG*, 13 November 1902, 2.

32. *NSJ*, 22 April 1913, 4.

33. *NSJ*, 20 December 1902, 8.

34. *NSJ*, 28 January 1903, 1; *Lyon County Times,* 7 February 1903, 6; *NSJ*, 14 June 1903, 3; 8 July 1903, 7; 25 November 1903, 8.

35. *NSJ*, 29 January 1903, 3.

36. *NSJ*, 21 February 1903, 4.

37. *NSJ*, 23 January 1903, 4; 14 June 1903, 3.

38. *REG*, 27 December 1902, 4; *NSJ*, 6 September 1905, 7.

39. *NSJ*, 24 January 1905, 5.

40. *REG*, 27 February 1906, 3.

41. *NSJ*, 10 April 1907, 7; *REG*, 24 January 1907, 7.

42. *NSJ*, 13 July 1912, 1; *REG*, 13 July 1912, 1 and 12.

43. *REG*, 13 July 1912, 12.

44. *REG*, 29 November 1912, 6; 29 October 1920, 8; 30 October 1920, 8.

45. *REG*, 29 July 1913, 1.

46. *NSJ*, 22 April 1913, 4; *REG*, 8 August 1913, 8.

47. Phillip I. Earl, "Railroads of Nevada," in the *Nevada Comprehensive Preservation*

*Plan,* 2nd ed., ed. William G. White, Ronald M. James, and Richard Bernstein (Carson City: Nevada Division of Historic Preservation and Archaeology, 1991).

48. *NSJ,* 18 September 1907, 4.

49. *NSJ,* 16 July 1929, 4.

50. Stornetta et al., *Reno Railroad Corridor,* 2.25.

51. *NSJ,* 14 November 1956, 3.

52. Braman B. Adams, *The Block System of Signaling on American Railroads* (New York: Railroad Gazette, 1901), 7.

53. Ibid.

54. "The Passing of the Semaphore," *Railway Age,* 15 February 1930, 420–21, reproduced in "Semaphore History" (Time-Consuming Productions, 1996–98), http://www.semaphores.com/resources/history/hist0598.html (accessed 15 February 2007).

55. Ibid.

56. *REG,* 25 November 1926, 3.

57. *NSJ,* 23 February 1905, 5.

58. Roy Curtis, Nevada Historical Society Photo Collection, Roy Curtis Collection no. 54, Man crossing tracks.

59. *REG,* 16 June 1923, 7.

60. *NSJ,* 1 October 1927, 8.

61. *REG,* 11 December 1928, 4.

62. *NSJ,* 21 November 1930, 8; 14 July 1957, 4; *REG,* 15 July 1957, 14.

63. *REG,* 17 July 1932, 10.

64. *REG,* 27 February 1957, 15.

65. *NSJ,* 16 July 1957, 4.

66. CPRR.org, "Rensselaer Iron Company 50 lb/yd. CPRR Rail, 1864," http://www.cprr.org/Museum/Ephemera/RIC_Rail_1864.html, last updated 1 January 2003 (accessed 24 March 2005).

67. *NSJ,* 18 October 1953, 14; 31 March 1954, 16.

68. Dan Edginton, personal communication to authors, 2003.

69. *REG,* 12 August 1881, 3.

## 4 | CITY INFRASTRUCTURE AND EVERYDAY LIFE

1. *NSJ,* 5 November 1873, 31.

2. Ibid.

3. Townley, *Tough Little Town on the Truckee,* 92.

4. Townley, *Tough Little Town on the Truckee,* states that the Depot Hotel burned down, but primary sources specify the extent of the damage and the fact that the hotel remained structurally intact; see *REG,* 13 February 1877, 3; *NSJ,* 14 February 1877, 1.

5. *REG,* 3 March 1879, 2.

6. Townley, *Tough Little Town on the Truckee,* 98.

7. Reno Fire Department, *History of the Reno Fire Department,* 83.

8. Stornetta et al., *Reno Railroad Corridor,* 2.22.

9. Townley, *Tough Little Town on the Truckee,* 80.

10. *NSJ,* 5 November 1873, 3.

11. *NSJ,* 2 September 1874, 3.

12. *REG,* 31 July 1876, 2.

13. *REG,* 7 October 1876, 1.

14. *RWG,* 4 March 1880, 6.

15. *REG,* 1 March 1883, 3.

16. *REG,* 2 February 1882, 3.

17. *REG,* 31 July 1876, 2.

18. *NSJ,* 3 October 1896, 6; *REG,* 20 July 1897, 3.

19. *NSJ,* 1 January 1902, 1.

20. *NSJ,* 15 March 1905, 8.

21. *NSJ,* 22 April 1951, 6:1–8.

22. Harold Curran, personal communication to Mary Ringhoff, 1 August 2003.

23. *NSJ,* 27 April 1897, 3.

24. Jacquelyn K. Sundstrand, "When Ditches Became Urban: Reno Women and the Fight to Prevent Child Deaths," *NHSQ* 47, no. 2 (2004): 115.

25. Ibid., 116; *NSJ,* 9 September 1954, 4; 3 March 1956, 14.

26. W. T. Holcomb (Reno Public Works Director), Correspondence to Louie Gardella (Washoe County Agricultural Agent) re: proposed elimination of the Sullivan-Kelly Ditch, 7 June 1967, Manuscript Collection 83-06, University of Nevada, Reno, Special Collections Department.

27. Townley, *Tough Little Town on the Truckee,* 80.

28. Ibid.

29. Ibid.

30. Ibid., 157.

31. Ibid., 158.

32. Stornetta et al., *Reno Railroad Corridor,* A-2; Townley, *Tough Little Town on the Truckee,* 158–59.

33. Townley, *Tough Little Town on the Truckee,* 269.

34. Camp, *Reno, Nevada,* map, 1879.

35. *REG,* 7 March 1907, 1.

36. Jon Schladweiler, Jan McDonald, Hale Burrus, Paul Matty, Stephanie Siva, Willie Hanson, Art Brandt, and Pete Corrao, "Pipes-wood (2)," Sewerhistory.org, http://www.sewerhistory.org/grfx/components/pipe-wood2.htm, last updated 2004 (accessed 20 January 2005).

37. *REG,* 6 October 1942, 8.

38. Stornetta et al., *Reno Railroad Corridor,* 2.22; Townley, *Tough Little Town on the Truckee,* 159.

39. Townley, *Tough Little Town on the Truckee,* 81; *NSJ,* 14 May 1887, 4.

40. *NSJ,* 15 February 1910, 8.

41. Townley, *Tough Little Town on the Truckee,* 81.

42. Ibid.

43. Peggy Trego, "Reno's First Electric Plant Had Capacity for 45 Lights," *NSJ*, 5 March 1950.

44. Ibid.

45. *NSJ*, 1 April 1950, 12.

46. Trego, "Reno's First Electric Plant Had Capacity for 45 Lights."

47. *NSJ*, 10 February 1957, 2.

48. *REG*, 4 October 1965, 10.

49. *NSJ*, 30 April 1957, 1.

50. *REG*, 6 October 1926, 8; 11 December 1926, 8.

51. *REG*, 20 March 1928, 7.

52. *REG*, 9 November 1934, 13.

53. *REG*, 19 October 1928, 9.

54. *REG*, 9 November 1934, 13.

55. *NSJ*, 2 May 1936, 8.

## 5 | THE STORY IN BROKEN BOTTLES

1. *REG*, 19 February 1900, 3.

2. John J. Riley, *A History of the American Soft Drink Industry: Bottled Carbonated Beverages, 1807–1957* (Washington, DC: American Bottlers of Carbonated Beverages, 1958), 161–62.

3. Ibid., 137.

4. Ibid., 133–35.

5. John R. Paul and Paul W. Parmalee, *Soft Drink Bottling: A History with Special Reference to Illinois* (Springfield: Illinois State Museum Society, 1973), 62.

6. M. L. Blumenthal, *The Bottler's Helper: A Practical Encyclopaedia for the Bottler of Soft Drinks Compiled from the Contributions of Over Seven Hundred Bottlers* (Philadelphia: Blumenthal Bros., 1907), 203–21.

7. Riley, *History of the American Soft Drink Industry*, 139.

8. Paul and Parmalee, *Soft Drink Bottling*, 67.

9. Harold T. Smith, "Prohibition in Nevada," *NHSQ* 18, no. 4 (1976): 234.

10. Rowley, *Reno: Hub of the Washoe Country*, 9.

11. Smith, "Prohibition in Nevada," 239.

12. Ibid., 243.

13. *Carson City Daily Appeal*, 11 October 1928, 2, in Smith, "Prohibition in Nevada," 245.

14. Harold Curran, personal communication to Mary Ringhoff, 1 August 2003.

15. David E. Kyvig, *Daily Life in the United States, 1920–1939: Decades of Promise and Pain* (Westport, CT: Greenwood Press, 2002), 151.

16. Riley, *History of the American Soft Drink Industry*, 147.

17. Rowley, *Reno: Hub of the Washoe Country*, 99.

18. Riley, *History of the American Soft Drink Industry*, 147.

19. Blumenthal, *The Bottler's Helper*, 155–85.

20. Jane Busch, "Second Time Around: A Look at Bottle Reuse," in *Approaches to*

*Material Culture Research for Historical Archaeologists,* 2nd ed., comp. David R. Brauner (Uniontown, PA: Society for Historical Archaeology, 2000), 179.

21. Riley, *History of the American Soft Drink Industry,* 147.

22. Busch, "Second Time Around," 184.

23. David Valentine, "Nehi in Debris: A Report on the Historic Artifact Collection from 26CK1278, Las Vegas Wash, Clark County, Nevada," prepared by HRA Conservation Archaeology, Inc., Las Vegas, 2005.

24. Ibid., 56.

25. *NSJ,* 17 December 1903, 10; *REG,* 17 April 1905, 8.

26. *NSJ,* 18 April 1905, 2.

27. Polk's City Business Directories, 1917 and 1920–21.

28. *NSJ,* 28 January 1910, 8.

29. Rowley, *Reno: Hub of the Washoe Country,* 99.

30. *NSJ,* 28 January 1910, 8; Sanborn Map and Publishing Company, *Reno, Nev.* fire insurance map (New York: Sanborn Map and Publishing Company, 1918).

31. *REG,* 4 August 1904, 8.

32. Riley, *History of the American Soft Drink Industry,* 181.

33. Ibid., 115.

34. Ibid., 134–36.

35. Paul and Parmalee, *Soft Drink Bottling,* 72.

36. Darla Potter, Notes on Frank Family History and Frank Bros. Bottling Works, unpublished genealogic research material, 2003.

37. William Hampton Adams, "Dating Historical Sites: The Importance of Understanding Time Lag in the Acquisition, Curation, Use, and Disposal of Artifacts," *Historical Archaeology* 37, no. 2 (2003): 38–64.

38. Darla Potter, personal communication to Mary Ringhoff, regarding Ed Folsom's recollections, 1 July 2003.

## 6 | AFRICAN AMERICAN–OWNED BUSINESSES IN THE LAKE-EVANS BLOCK

1. Elmer Rusco, *"Good Time Coming?": Black Nevadans in the Nineteenth Century* (Westport, CT: Greenwood Press, 1975), 124–26.

2. Ibid., 124.

3. Ibid.; Michael Coray, "African-Americans in Nevada," *NHSQ* 35, no. 4 (1995): 239.

4. *NSJ,* 22 November 1904, in Elmer Rusco, *"Good Time Coming?,"* 209.

5. *NSJ,* 28 December 1924, 6.

6. Elmer Rusco with R. T. King, *Not Like a River: The Memoir of an Activist Academic* (Reno: University of Nevada Oral History Program, 2004), in Guy Rocha, "The Mississippi of the West," *Nevada Observer* 2, no. 19 (1 August 2005) (originally published in *Sierra Sage,* Carson City/Carson Valley, Nevada, August 2006 edition).

7. Onie Cooper, personal communication to Mary Ringhoff, 21 September 2007.

8. Dolores Feemster, personal communication to Mary Ringhoff, 25 May 2007.

9. Norma Washington, personal communication to Mary Ringhoff, 15 August 2007.

10. Bureau of Governmental Research, *Voices of Black Nevada* (Reno: Bureau of Governmental Research, University of Nevada, Elmer R. Rusco, Director, 1971), 46. Charles Mapes owned the Mapes Hotel, the most famous hotel in Reno and the venue for many city social events; the Mapes was infamous in the black community for refusing service to blacks.

11. Rocha, "The Mississippi of the West."

12. Ibid.

13. Paul A. Shackel, "Archaeology, Memory, and Landscapes of Conflict," *Historical Archaeology* 37, no. 3 (2003): 3–13; Eric L. Larsen, "Integrating Segregated Urban Landscapes of the Late-Nineteenth and Early-Twentieth Centuries," *Historical Archaeology* 37, no. 3 (2003): 111–23.

14. Shackel, "Archaeology, Memory, and Landscapes of Conflict," 3.

15. Albin J. Cofone, "Reno's Little Italy: Italian Entrepreneurship and Culture in Northern Nevada," *NHSQ* 26, no. 2 (1983): 103.

16. *NSJ*, 4 August 1878, 1.

17. *REG*, 2 November 1908, 1; Rowley, *Reno: Hub of the Washoe Country*, 46.

18. Harold Curran, personal communication to Mary Ringhoff, 1 August 2003.

19. Robbins E. Cahill, *Robbins E. Cahill: Recollections of Work in State Politics, Government, Taxation, Gaming Control, Clark County Administration, and the Nevada Resort Association (Part 1)* (interviewed by Mary Ellen Glass) (Reno: Oral History Program, University of Nevada, 1977), 50.

20. Cofone, "Reno's Little Italy," 103.

21. *NSJ*, 6 August 1907, 8.

22. *NSJ*, 5 August 1907, 5.

23. Rusco, *"Good Time Coming?,"* 129.

24. *NSJ*, 28 December 1924, 6.

25. David Love, personal communication to Mary Ringhoff, 25 July 2005; *NSJ*, 9 December 1933, 1.

26. Andrew Ginocchio, *Andrew Ginocchio: The Ascent of Reno Iron Works* (interviewed by R. T. King) (Reno: Oral History Program, University of Nevada, 1987), 71.

27. *NSJ*, 10 November 1932, 3.

28. *NSJ*, 3 June 1932, 8.

29. *REG*, 26 January 1933, 2.

30. *REG*, 9 December 1933, 12.

31. *REG*, 27 December 1933, 2.

32. *REG*, 13 January 1937.

33. *NSJ*, 23 February 1949, 13.

34. *REG*, 23 November 1937, 2.

35. *REG*, 28 April 1944, 11.

36. *REG*, 20 November 1940, 12.

37. *REG*, 25 September 1945, 11.

38. *NSJ*, 9 March 1948, 5.

39. *REG*, 9 March 1948.

40. Unless noted otherwise, biographical information on Bill Bailey comes from

"The Life of William Bailey," an unpublished document in the University of Nevada, Reno, Special Collections, NC 18/I/12, confirmed by Bailey on 10 December 1960.

41. Albert W. Moe, *Nevada's Golden Age of Gambling* (Canada: Puget Sound Books, 2001), 43.

42. *NSJ*, 8 February 1945, 16.

43. Onie Cooper, personal communication to Mary Ringhoff, 21 September 2007.

44. *NSJ*, 12 October 1949, 16.

45. Onie Cooper, personal communication to Mary Ringhoff, 21 September 2007.

46. *NSJ*, 13 October 1955, 12; *REG*, 1 November 1955, 3.

47. *NSJ*, 17 February 1956, 22.

48. *NSJ*, 11 October 1956.

49. Moe, *Nevada's Golden Age of Gambling*, 43; *NSJ*, 22 June 1960, 27.

50. Dwayne Kling, *The Rise of the Biggest Little City: An Encyclopedic History of Reno Gaming, 1931–1981* (Reno: University of Nevada Press, 2000), 61.

51. *NSJ*, 3 July 1971, 6.

52. *NSJ*, 1 July 1971, 1.

53. *NSJ*, 21 September 1974, 4.

54. *NSJ*, 12 June 1957, 18; 21 June 1957, 10.

55. Oteria Cole, personal communication to Mary Ringhoff, 5 July 2005.

56. *REG*, 6 January 1959, 35.

57. *NSJ*, 12 January 1972, 2.

58. *REG*, 19 April 1945.

59. Dolores Feemster, personal communication to Mary Ringhoff, 25 May 2007.

60. *REG*, 10 January 1946, 19.

61. Cahill, *Robbins E. Cahill*, 58.

62. Lai King Chew, *Lai King Chew: The Cosmo Club and Reno's Chinese Community* (interviewed by Hwa-di Brodhead and Michael Brodhead) (Reno: University of Nevada Oral History Program, 2000), 28–29.

63. Nevada State Legislature, Senate Concurrent Resolution no. 27, Memorializing Civil Rights Leader Bertha Woodard, minutes, 3 April 2001, http://www.leg.state.nv.us/71st/Journal/Senate/Final/sj058.html, accessed 27 June 2003.

64. *REG*, 14 December 1949.

65. Wayne Crawford, personal communication to Mary Ringhoff, 26 August 2003.

66. Oteria Cole, personal communication to Mary Ringhoff, 5 July 2005.

67. Onie Cooper, personal communication to Mary Ringhoff, 21 September 2007.

68. Rosemary Peacock, *The Black Experience in the Silver State* (DVD; Reno: KNPB Channel 5 Public Broadcasting, 1993).

69. Oteria Cole, personal communication to Mary Ringhoff, 5 July 2005.

70. Cage Byrd, "Southern Pacific Right of Way and Adjacent Area Personal Property Department," sketches and notes, Washoe County Assessor's Office, book 59, 1963; Wayne Crawford, personal communication to Mary Ringhoff, 26 August 2003; Oteria Cole, personal communication to Mary Ringhoff, 5 July 2005.

71. Chew, *Lai King Chew*, 32–33.

72. Ibid.

73. Ibid., 42–43.

74. James B. McMillan, *Fighting Back: A Life in the Struggle for Civil Rights* (interviewed by Gary E. Elliott, narrative interpretation by R. T. King) (Reno: University of Nevada Oral History Program, 1997), 138.

75. Chew, *Lai King Chew,* 33–34.

76. Cahill, *Robbins E. Cahill,* 55.

77. Norma Washington and Dolores Feemster, personal communication to Mary Ringhoff, 15 August 2007.

78. Lubertha Johnson, *Lubertha Johnson: Civil Rights Efforts in Las Vegas: 1940s–1960s* (edited by Jamie Coughtry and R. T. King) (Reno: University of Nevada Oral History Program, 1988), 31.

79. Wayne Crawford, personal communication to Mary Ringhoff, 26 August 2003.

80. McMillan, *Fighting Back,* 139.

81. Johnson, *Lubertha Johnson,* 66.

82. Chew, *Lai King Chew,* 62–63.

83. Sanborn Map and Publishing Company, *Reno, Nev. April 1890,* fire insurance map (New York: Sanborn Map and Publishing Company, 1890); *Reno, Nev. April 1899,* fire insurance map (New York: Sanborn Map and Publishing Company, 1899).

84. Sanborn Map and Publishing Company, *Reno, Nev. May 1904,* fire insurance map (New York: Sanborn Map and Publishing Company, 1904), *Reno, Nev. 1918,* fire insurance map (New York: Sanborn Map and Publishing Company, 1918), 1933 hand-pasted revisions to 1918 map.

85. Chew, *Lai King Chew,* 38–39.

## CONCLUSION

1. Alicia Barber, *Reno's Big Gamble: Image and Reputation in the Biggest Little City* (Lawrence: University Press of Kansas, 2008).

2. Ibid., 6.

3. Ibid., 7.

4. Townley, *Tough Little Town on the Truckee,* xiii.

5. Thomas, "Archaeologies of Place and Landscape," 173.

6. Max Miller, *Reno,* 31–32.

# Index